BUILDING
A CHILD'S
LIBRARY

BUILDING A CHILD'S LIBRARY

Inside Twenty-Five Classic Children's Stories

Miriam J. Johnson

Paulist Press
New York/Mahwah, N.J.

Book and cover design by Lynn Else

Copyright © 2004 by Miriam J. Johnson

All rights reserved. No part of this book may be reproduced or transmitted in any form or by any means, electronic or mechanical, including photocopying, recording or by any information storage and retrieval system without permission in writing from the Publisher.

Library of Congress Cataloging-in-Publication Data

Johnson, Miriam, 1932-
    Building a child's library : inside twenty-five classic children's stories / Miriam J. Johnson.
        p. cm.
    ISBN 0-8091-4229-5 (alk. paper)
    1. Children—Books and reading—United States. 2. Children's literature—Stories, plots, etc. 3. Children's literature, American—Bibliography. 4. Religious education of children. 5. Values in literature. I. Title.
    Z1037.A1 J68 2004
    028.5'5—dc22

                                                    2003016513

Published by Paulist Press
997 Macarthur Boulevard
Mahwah, New Jersey 07430

www.paulistpress.com

Printed and bound in the
United States of America

Contents

For my granddaughter

Rebecca Elizabeth Johnson

Preface

When the opportunity came to write once again on values in children's literature, I was delighted. My first two books, *Inside Twenty-Five Classic Children's Stories: Discovering Values at Home or in School,* volumes 1 and 2, were published decades ago. Since then there have been so many stellar children's books, from a more diverse, more exciting perspective, that it was like a wonderful feast of gourmet food from which to choose.

As in the first two volumes, I envision children of preschool through elementary school ages reading the selected books either by themselves or with parents, grandparents, teachers, or older siblings. This book contains summaries, commentaries, and suggestions for conversation starters to be used by the adults or older siblings as a kind of background.

The books referred to are to be enjoyed by all ages. And, as I emphatically stated in the other prefaces, BOOKS ARE, FIRST AND FOREMOST, TO BE ENJOYED. It would make me very sad if I knew this book prompted long, drawn out, didactic discussions about what some call "lessons to be learned from books."

I have seen that kind of preachy/teachy approach discourage many young students from reading further. As a former classroom teacher, a school librarian, and a parent and grandparent, I have observed children get excited over books for the sheer pleasure of savoring them—and that is a coveted end result.

I found there were times when just a comment such as, "Isn't that awesome that God had a design in which no two snowflakes are alike!" could awaken the young reader to the realization that God still has a hand in this world. Thinking about God's care and connections could be a natural one—not a forced one with pat answers to questions or "socially acceptable" responses that usually do not reflect a reader's real thoughts.

1

I have suggested "Conversation Starters" merely as ideas for reflecting on the stories if it seems an appropriate time. Never feel as if you have to use all of them. Moreover, you, as a parent or teacher or someone involved in children's lives in a different role, might have other motivating thoughts. And, sometimes, the reading of the story might be sufficient, without any conversations.

After reading many quality books I finally decided on twenty-five and categorized them under the headings *Creature Connections, God's Care and Forgiveness, Justice for All, World Religions,* and *Music.* While these designations are not mutually exclusive, I felt upon reading and rereading the books that they had these themes in common.

I avoided labeling the books for preschool, for grade 1, and so on. As a former classroom teacher, school librarian, and member of the Reading Department in a large public school system, I know that children vary in their interests and reading skills. I have seen fifth graders enjoy and become enlightened by picture books, so who am I to declare that a certain book ought to be used only by second graders? I have given the number of pages (counting the pages in books with no pagination!) as a bit of a reference on how long or involved the "read" might be.

Finally, it is my hope that these carefully culled books can bring meaningful and significant moments to the lives of younger and older readers alike. Whether the books are read together or separately, there just might be a time that thoughts can be shared in an open and nonthreatening way—a way in which God's care and forgiveness comes through to us.

Creation Connections

One Flake at a Time

Snowflake Bentley

by Jacqueline Briggs Martin

illustrated by Mary Azarian

32 pages

(Boston: Houghton Mifflin, 1998)

> *Wilson Bentley was born with a desire that no one else had,
> as far as we know. He wanted to take pictures of snowflakes,
> and when he was finally able to, he discovered what no other
> human being before him had known. Now we know and it is
> an awesome thing to contemplate.*

How many snowflakes does it take to make a mound of
snow at one end of a mall's parking lot? What's even more amazing is that, whatever the number, no two snowflakes are identical. We go down hills of snow on sleds and skis. We dig tunnels
in it and in the north we shovel it, but we can know all this without pondering that no two snowflakes are the same or what this
means.

Wilson Bentley was born on February 9, 1865, in Jericho,
Vermont, where the annual snowfall is 120 inches. For some reason he loves the snow, and he is aware that, whatever the amount
of snow, it is made up of individual flakes. Yet try as he might he
can never take one flake anywhere before it melts. He can catch

butterflies in a net and show them to his friends. He can carry an apple blossom to his mother, but not a snowflake.

He tells his mother of his desire to see what a snowflake looks like and she responds by giving him an old microscope. He places drops of water under the microscope and blades of grass. He is fascinated by what he sees, but what he wants so much to see he can never see—a snowflake, just one. He wants to draw one but it always melts before he finishes. He learns that most of them have six branches or arms, each of which is the same as the other five, but for three years he tries to draw one and cannot do it before it melts.

At age sixteen he reads about a microscope that has a built-in camera. If only he had it he would not have to draw snowflakes anymore. He could take their picture. He either pestered his parents about this, or something else moved them to do so, but one year later they use their savings to buy Wilson this camera/microscope. It cost his father as much as his herd of cows, but it is powerful enough to magnify a snowflake up to 3,600 times its actual size. At first he still has trouble with them melting but eventually he learns how to deal with this.

Every so often one hears about parents who see some special interest a son or daughter has and they encourage it. This usually means spending some money, but it sounds as if in Wilson Bentley's case his parents both see and appreciate this special interest, and then go the extra mile to support him.

With the new microscope, information always known to God begins to enter his awareness also. Each flake begins as a speck, too tiny to see with the naked eye. But as water attaches to the speck, it grows and forms these six branches. All six are alike on any one speck. As the branches enlarge they send out connecting links of crystal to the other branches with the result that the spaces between the six branches and their links are exactly the same size. However, the overall design of each flake is different from any other that Bentley saw.

The shape the flake takes depends on the temperature, the differences in wind, or the presence of moisture, but in this book this is as far as the author goes in describing the fact that no two snowflakes are the same.

A winter could go by and he might get only twelve good pictures, but in February 1928, there is a two-day snowstorm in Vermont and he succeeds in getting 100 pictures. He keeps all these pictures and it is from this number that he draws the conclusion that no two are alike, and probably never will be.

He makes special pictures of snowflakes and gives them away as gifts. He makes them into slides and projects them onto sheets hanging on clotheslines, much to the delight of children and other friends. Word spreads and colleges and universities buy copies of his photographs, and each year add them to their collections. He becomes famous as the Snowflake Man, but he never becomes rich. Any money he makes he spends on more pictures. When he is sixty, his photos are published in a book. Thirty days later, after walking six miles through a blizzard, he gets sick and two weeks later he dies.

It seems safe to assume that the number of different designs in snowflakes are infinite, meaning they are beyond numbering, like the stars in the sky or the grains of sand on a beach.

If we pick up where the book leaves off, we would first point out that there are only two alternatives to explaining something like this: chance or design. If chance explains this snowflake phenomenon, it appears that even in chance there is a design that prevents duplicates from ever happening.

The moment we eliminate chance as a rational explanation for the seemingly infinite variety in snowflakes, however, we must turn to design, and when we do that we enter a theological realm, meaning a realm where God is at work.

Anything with design means thought has been given to it, and there is no such thing as a thought without a thinker, and in this case, the word "Thinker" begins with a capital T, which makes the word stand for God.

To keep chance from duplicating the design requires an infinite kind of power capable of building into the snowflake equation a guideline that never slows down, takes a break, or ceases. It is on infinite alert.

That an infinite variation in snowflakes would point to the Creator is not exactly surprising. It's just never been said before. Not even Snowflake Bentley said it in his book, but it would seem to be the driving force in this singular individual. God used him as the vehicle through whom God reveals this amazing phenomenon: there are no two snowflakes exactly alike. It's like human fingerprints, only the signature here is that of the Author of Life, not one of his human writers.

Conversation Starters

1. What were the turning points in Wilson's life?

2. Where did his unique interest in snowflakes come from?

3. What meaning do you see in no two snowflakes being identical?

4. How do you feel about chance as the explanation for why there are no two snowflakes alike?

5. How would chance serve as the explanation for why there are no two fingerprints alike?

6. What reason might God have for introducing an infinite number of different snowflakes into the world?

Appalachia: The Voices of Sleeping Birds

by Cynthia Rylant

illustrated by Barry Moser

32 pages

(New York: Harcourt Brace, 1991)

> *The people who live in Appalachia are part of the mountains. They live on them and work in them, quite literally, mining coal. Upon them we were once dependent for warmth in the winter. Some still are. To the people of Appalachia the Source is God.*

Today many people still use coal to heat their homes. Up until around 1950 I, too, lived in a house warmed by coal in the winter months. My mother cooked on a coal stove. A few times a year the coal truck would make a delivery. It would back up to a basement window, push it open, and insert a metal chute from the truck through the window and into a room below called a coal bin.

Then the thunder rolled even on a cloudless day. As the lumps of coal slid down the chute and landed on the cement floor, the noise was deafening, especially if you were a child peering into the cellar. After the delivery was completed, there

9

was coal dust everywhere. You could write your name in it on the floor.

We knew what we were getting, but we did not have the faintest idea who made it possible for us to receive it. Yet we were dependent upon whoever they were for warmth when it was cold outside. That is still true now when oil or gas heats our homes. We do not know the people who refine it and keep it coming to us.

In *Appalachia: The Voices of Sleeping Birds,* Cynthia Rylant provides us with a rich resource on the folks who heat(ed) our homes. The coal camps of Appalachia are nestled in a stretch of mountains that run north and south from Pennsylvania to Tennessee like the back of a very long dinosaur who lay down to take a nap. Her description of the people's voices as those of sleeping birds is particularly apropos.

Many of the people live in tiny dwellings made of wood or brick. Some have new cars parked alongside. Others have just parts of cars in their yards. Most have running water for sinks and bathrooms, but some have to carry water to their houses and use outhouses for toilet facilities. However, whatever their houses are made of, the outside walls are covered with a thick layer of coal dust. Like our basement floor after a coal delivery, you can trace a picture on these walls, but unlike our floor dust, their wall dust hardens underneath like a coat of black paint.

The people of Appalachia have lived there for generations, and mining is all most of them know, thanks to the mountains. A few leave the area to become doctors or teachers but even they usually return and cannot say why. Those who never leave speak of a certain fear of going beyond the mountains. Their security is in the peaks and valleys, partly because they are "full of coal which people want." While going beyond the mountains makes them apprehensive, traveling two miles deep inside them is something the men do all week to get the coal. Mornings in Appalachia are "quiet and full of light." The mountains "look new, like God made them just that day." Nights are thick with darkness and the coal camps are often covered with a layer of fog.

The seasons of the year are important to Appalachian families. In the summer the men repair fences and tend to their gardens so their wives have fruits and vegetables to can later for the winter months. In the fall the men enjoy sitting on their porches in rocking chairs and staring at the mountains that surround them. The children like all the seasons. Living in the mountains makes them feel important. Perhaps teachers keep them informed of what their families are contributing to life in the United States. The children also think of God because they see what God has done in the creation of mountains and coal.

The people of Appalachia are religious people, meaning they go to church regularly on Sunday mornings and some go back in the evening. They go to Roman Catholic, Baptist, Methodist, or Presbyterian churches.

Whatever their church connection, they have something in common. They don't talk about God much. On this subject their voices are like sleeping birds. However, that does not mean they do not *think* about God. An important point in the book, almost poignant, is the fact that "most of them are thinkers, because these mountains inspire that, but they could never find the words to tell you of these thoughts they have." Were you to drive through the mountains and stop to say hello, or even to stay a while, they would "talk to you of their corn or their cows instead and keep the [more serious] thoughts to themselves."

When a reader puts together the regular attendance at church and this inability to say what they think, it leads to the possibility that they do not express their religious thoughts because their preachers do that for them. Whatever someone else does for us can impede us from learning how to do it for ourselves. Thus, the Appalachian people may talk of cows and

11

corn—small talk—while inside their heads are some very important words that remain part of the Appalachians' great unsaid.

Whether the outside voice of the preachers and the inside voice of the people match, we do not know. Still, were we to imagine what might be going through their minds it is not hard. They just might be pondering the part they as people play in the scheme of things, at least here in America. Native Americans lived in tepees for thousands of years, but those of us whose ancestors came from Europe know only how to live in houses. The Indians were accustomed to the cold, but Europeans, especially the northern Europeans, had to have warmth in their "tepees" in order to survive. And it was the role of the Appalachian mountain people to provide for this necessity for people all over America. Some coal came from surface mines in the Midwest, but most of it came from deep in the ground and from the people who were willing to travel down there to get it. The coal miners might have thought of this when they sat on their porches and "stared at the mountains."

They might also have had an even deeper thought. Who put the idea in a human being's head that there was something deep inside the mountains that could be burned and used to heat houses? Where would the idea come from that people should start digging for something? The Puritans came from Europe but they burned wood. They did not know about coal. And even if they did, that just pushes the question from the United States to Europe. Was the original impulse or "gut feeling" that there was something there one that was itself planted by the Creator (who alone knew it was there)? If newcomers to America needed warmth someone or something had to provide it. Perhaps the most awesome Source begins with a capital S.

Conversation Starters

1. If you are an older reader, can you recall or describe the experience of having coal brought to your house?

2. Mountains fill many people with awe, but what further thoughts might the miners from Appalachia have?

3. Where do you think the first human being to decide to dig in the earth for coal got the idea?

4. What do you think about the idea that listening to preachers do most of the talking about God forces many of us to keep our thoughts about God inside our heads?

Out of the Dust

by Karen Hesse

240 pages

(New York: Scholastic, 1997)

> *Billy Joe and Job would have had a lot to talk about. Both of them were characters in stories that might cause readers to wonder if there is such a thing as God's care and concern. In Billy Joe's case, the passage of time was a help.*

This book is a sobering read. At least it was for me. However, realizing it was a Newbery Award winner, I knew others were convinced it was one of the best books written for children that year. Also, I liked the unique style of using prose-poetry and the way the author designated the months and years at the beginning of each chapter and at the end of each selection.

The reader is introduced to life in an Oklahoma dust bowl when Billy Joe's mother asks her to set the table. It is the same for every meal. Plates, cups, and glasses are placed upside down for each member of the family. Doing it that way helps keep them from eating and drinking dust along with the food. Still, her dad observes how there is pepper on the potatoes and the milk is chocolate, but in reality the pepper and chocolate are simply dust.

One way Billy Joe lives with the dust is by playing the piano with her mother, who is her piano teacher. To Billy Joe, "my place in the world is at the piano," and she earns a little money doing it even though she is only fourteen. She loves to "pester the keys."

The first month around which the story pivots is July 1934, when a terrible catastrophe occurs in the kitchen. Her father sets a pail of kerosene beside the stove, which her mother thinks is water and begins pouring into the coffee pot on the stove. It becomes a rope of fire that burns her mother badly. The father rigs up a tent over the bed so nothing will touch her because she is in such pain, but she soon dies. Her death fills Billy Joe with anger, partly because her own hands were burned in the incident so she cannot play the piano. She claims she will never forgive her father for causing the catastrophe. Accidents are called accidents because they usually are not preventable. They just happen. Nonetheless, it takes time for Billy Joe to stop blaming her father, just over a year according to the story's dateline.

The low point in the book for me is when shortly after this disaster grasshoppers invade the area, eating everything, crops, grass, and the apples on the tree Billy Joe's mother had been caring for. Two cores are left on the tree. This brings back memories to me of living in southwestern Iowa during the Depression years when my father was pastor in a rural parish there. We had dust storms and droughts but never to the extent that Billy Joe experienced in Oklahoma.

It seems that dust is always around, seeping into the house even between the three major storms that are recorded in this book. The first comes in January 1935 and is so bad the farmers have to kill their cows because they cannot drink water since the dust fills their nostrils and mouths. This is followed by rain, but it is not enough to wash the dust away so it turns into mud and has to be scraped away.

The second major dust storm arrives in March 1935. Dust plugs Billy Joe's nose and collects inside her mouth so that no matter how hard she presses her lips together "the dust makes muddy tracks across her tongue." Then, one month later, they have another big storm. They are on the road when it hits. When they return home "the front door hung open blown in by the wind. Dust lay two feet deep in rippling waves across the parlor floor." It covers the stove, icebox, and kitchen chairs. And her piano is buried in it.

As I read, I began looking for what could be called "hints of hope." The first hint starts in September 1934, two months after the accident, when her father begins digging a huge hole that he believes will someday soon be filled with water thanks to rain. Then in January 1935 Billy Joe hears her father singing. His voice "starts and stops like a car short of gas," but it is singing. This comes halfway through the book. Another hint occurs in February 1935, when Billy Joe tries to play the piano and wins third prize in a talent contest. However, it leaves her hands in great pain, so she decides never to play again. One month later her father starts attending night school, and that month Billy Joe decides she wants to live. She had all but given up on that idea after her mother died.

In May 1935 in a selection entitled "Hope" it rains—a lot. The hole her father dug fills with water and is called a pond. The rain also helps to bring back grass. The reader may recall how Billy Joe's father had commenced digging the hole in September, so eight months later his belief in rain comes true. A selection labeled "Hope Smothered" follows and with it the dust returns.

In August of that summer Billy Joe decides to get out of the dust, despite the hints of hope and rain. She hops a train for the West Coast. On the train she meets a father who cannot bear to watch his wife and children suffer from the drought, and then she realizes her father is made of stronger stuff. He is "more like sod. Steady, silent, and deep. Holding on to life, with reserves underneath to sustain him, and me, and anyone else who came near." Billy Joe decides then to go back home. It is also at this point, over a year since the accident, that she first feels like forgiving her father.

The story ends on a further positive note with Billy Joe going to the doctor and learning that if she plays the piano and stretches her hands they will eventually be much better. Her father meets another woman at night school and she, too, becomes a welcome part of their lives.

Conversation Starters

1. Was there a low point in the story for you?

2. Were there other signs of hope that you noticed?

3. What does this story tell us about God's care?

When Sophie Gets Angry— Really, Really Angry

by Molly Bang

40 pages

(New York: The Blue Sky Press, 1999)

> *Anger is a human emotion that in different degrees shows itself at some point in perhaps everybody. Unlike perhaps everybody, Sophie has a fixed way of dealing with it. It's a kind of ritual that works for her. What she does not realize is that the Creator is also working with her at the same time.*

Anger is introduced at the beginning of this book, but most of the book is about the great outdoors and what it does to relieve Sophie of her anger. Many children enjoy playing outdoors and experience some of the same mental medicine without realizing it.

What gets Sophie's dander up is when both she and her sister want to play with a stuffed animal at the same time, and her mother tells Sophie it is her sister's turn. It is this that gets Sophie in such a rage that "she kicks. She screams. She wants to smash the world to smithereens." "She roars a red, red roar" and the picture (all the excellent illustrations are done by the author) to show this is a loud, almost fiery burst of energy escaping from Sophie's lips and blowing things over inside her house in the process.

Sophie is a volcano, ready to explode, and when she gets angry—really angry—she does what may seem like an unusual thing: she runs. "She runs and runs and runs until she can't run anymore."

Parents who routinely incorporate exercise into their lives, such as swimming, biking, running, or aerobics, may want to explain to their children that by running, one of the things Sophie does is cause her brain to secrete a chemical that floods her whole being with a calming, rejuvenating feeling. My daughter used to do this in college. When she was blue or stressed out for some reason, she would go for a run, and she always came back to her dorm refreshed, a new person.

When Sophie tires of running, she has quite the opposite reaction for a moment or two. She cries. However, this only lasts for one page, and as soon as her eyes clear she begins to drink in and enjoy what is around her. Trees and plants come into view, and she even hears a bird. She is becoming a nature person.

Familiar territory also lifts her spirits. She reaches an old beech tree laying on its side and easily climbs onto it. She perches on a limb like the bird she hears, and she feels the breeze blow her hair. She watches the water and the waves of the nearby sea, something thousands of seashore vacationers pay money to do near a camp for a week or two. Again there is a sympathetic tie between Sophie and the view from the tree, of which she is one part. As she gazes at the sea, the sea gives something to her.

For Sophie, the outdoors becomes a comfort zone. What the author does not verbalize is that Sophie has entered that place in the physical world where the Creator's specialties are reaching out to her. She is graced by their features and cannot help being lifted by them.

Thus the time comes when Sophie climbs down from the tree and "feels better now," so she "heads for home."

The story states that her home is warm and smells good when she enters the front door, implying that she perhaps is entertaining a chill as the breeze flew through the tree, and her mother might be preparing a meal.

What is equally pleasant is that "everyone is glad she's home," including her sister. "Everything's back together again." The family puzzle is literally and figuratively a picture of peace, and "Sophie isn't angry anymore."

In reading this book one is reminded of or becomes aware of how the setting for this story is conducive for Sophie's escape therapy. Children whose lawns are asphalt, and who never see, smell, or roll in grass, also experience anger, but the Creator's natural medicine is not there to assist them, unless they live near a park.

They can still run though.

Conversation Starters

1. When do you get most angry?

2. What do you do about it?

3. Has anger ever helped you?

Joseph Had a Little Overcoat

by Simms Taback

32 pages

(New York: Viking /Penguin, 1999)

> *Talk about shriveling down. How about an overcoat being used to cover a button? And if you think the title has anything to do with the coat of Joseph in the Bible, forget it. There is no connection.*

That's true! The coat the biblical Joseph receives from his father, Jacob, which leads to a peck of trouble with his brothers, is a coat of many colors. The coat of the Joseph this book is about is drab. There's no Technicolor Dream Coat here. The fabric remnants that fill the end papers inside the covers are far more beautiful than the overcoat in the story. And the color of the coat never changes. Only the shape changes, seven times, until the last bit of fabric used to cover the button disappears when the owner, who happens to be a tailor, loses it. The words *Joseph* and *overcoat* that form parts of the title are similar to the biblical tale in name only.

Actually without this Joseph being a tailor, it would be hard to tell this tale, because seven times he uses needle and thread to make the story go someplace.

In the beginning, Joseph the tailor sews himself an overcoat. It looks fairly good for quite a while, but then threads begin hanging down from the bottom of the coat, and it is just a matter of time before the whole coat takes on a ragged appearance. However, being a tailor, he is creative. He snips and sews and turns the overcoat into a jacket.

It too wears out, and probably faster than the original overcoat since it is made from the same material and that material, having been around a while, has already been worn down some. But the tailor keeps clipping and snipping, using whatever material is still whole to make something smaller.

That's the way the story goes. Seven times he does his thing, and each time what he makes out of the cloth allows him to go someplace and do something fun. Even when the material left can only be made into a handkerchief, he uses it for a bib, so the drops from hot tea that spill on it won't burn his neck. You have to give the old man credit. He has resourcefulness and creativity coming out of his pores.

So does the Caldecott-winning author/illustrator, Simms Taback. On each page there is a die-cut hole in the paper. Upon turning the page, what should appear but the original material in its new shape and with its new purpose!

In a way, Joseph is battling with time. This is something that manufacturers in America count on. They build into their products what is called "planned obsolescence," which is a fancy way of saying that in due time most things wear out and have to be replaced. It's just that if you plan it, things wear out faster.

Throwing out what's no longer wanted is one step removed from planned obsolescence. Like some kind of virus that has entered society, there is a strain that opts for just getting rid of whatever doesn't work or fit anymore. Things are disposable. We are told that it is cheaper to buy a certain kind of camera, aim it and shoot, and, after removing the picture, throw the whole thing away. Amazing!

Then there are toys, tons of toys. They litter the floor, so you may not be able to see the carpet or the floor boards. At an early age some kids have so many toys that when they step on them and they break, they throw them away and buy new ones, just like the cameras and razors.

When I was a child my folks didn't have money for lots of toys, so we took good care of them, and when they broke we fixed them. We learned not to be wasteful. Today some kids are learning the same thing but in a new way. They discover that when a new toy comes at holiday or birthday time, it lasts for a while—the fun, that is—and then it seems to get old, not the paint or the parts but the fun. Things like toys can soon find their way into a box where they sit unused.

Perhaps kids grow out of them, or perhaps kids—some kids—know that things cost money, and what is the point of paying out money for something that just doesn't last? We've observed our grandchildren having fun making something and then playing with it. In fact, the process of building something may be where the fun is. It's as if being the inventor gives back its own brand of satisfaction, and whether they realize how they have beat the system, that is what they have done. They have broken the cycle.

Of course, the word *cycle* conjures up the term *recycle*. We are into that too. Stores will refund a nickel for each empty aluminum can as an incentive. However, the satisfaction doesn't really come from the nickels that tumble out of the recycling machine. It comes from knowing that it can take an estimated 500 years for an aluminum can to biodegrade in a dump, whereas recycle it and it can be back on the shelf in sixty days. The machine crushes them and the can manufacturer melts them down, refashions the molten metal into a new can, and, when refilled, we may be buying our old can. We have no way of knowing that but we can know and believe that we are conserving metal. We are not being wasteful.

That seems to be the point of *Joseph Had a Little Overcoat*. He is by trade or nature not willing to waste the material that goes into his original coat. So he recycles it. He used it again and again, until his seventh effort. Still, even though he had nothing left, he wrote a story about it. He even ended up making something out of nothing!

Let's hear it for Joseph, for buttons, for thrift, for recycling, for creativity, for storytelling...and more.

Conversation Starters

1. Are we really as wasteful as it seems we are?

2. What, if anything, do you recycle—paper, oil, cans, glass, toys?

3. Which of Joseph's seven recyclings struck you as the best?

4. Have some fun with the Yiddish folksong at the end of the story.

Chato's Kitchen

by Gary Soto

illustrated by Susan Guevara

32 pages

(New York: Putnam, 1995)

> *Beneath the veneer of Spanish language, humor, and a clever plot, there is something serious going on in this story about mice, cats, and a dog all ending up at the same dinner party.*

The pictures and words evoke mirth, but even in the first page Chato the cat has a sinister look as he contemplates having a sparrow for lunch. He investigates some noise next door only to discover a whole family of juicy mice moving in. Suddenly, his mealtime prospects multiply. In what is a clever play on words, he decides to "invite them for dinner." Even if he had said he would *have* them for dinner it would have been the same result, whether spoken in barrio Spanish or colloquial English.

All the characters in this plot speak Spanish, so there is a sprinkling of such words in italics, immediately followed when they are used by the English equivalents in parentheses.

The menu, that is, the mice, accept the dinner invitation and recall that a friend by the name of Chorizo is coming over to visit them that evening. They inform Chato that they are bringing a guest along.

Chato immediately thinks his dinner has now become five mice, along with side dishes such as fajitas, salsa, and enchiladas. When a cat friend of his stops by, he agrees to stay and help with the feast. The two go to work and Chato's menu, printed in the front of the book, becomes the focus of their culinary attention.

The doorbell rings, signaling the arrival of the dinner guests—and dinner. With their eyes spelling s-i-n-i-s-t-e-r and their stomachs in a roar, Chato and his cat friend open the door only to find a huge dog standing there with an equally sinister set of eyes. The mice family is riding comfortably on his back. The cats scramble for the curtain and a quick climb to safety. Mami (mama) mouse assures them the dog is cat-friendly, but you would never know from the looks on their faces. Slowly everyone takes their seats, and the dinner begins. Chato knows he is not going to be eating any guests that evening. Whether *he* might become the meal is his new concern.

We are perhaps all acquainted with the fear mice have of cats, and the similar fear most cats have of dogs. Perhaps it runs in the animal family. Size in the animal kingdom seems to determine status, though there are exceptions, and perhaps there are myths.

A friend of our daughter has some cats. One afternoon a woodpecker flew headfirst into her closed window. She was on her feet in a flash and brought the bird into the house. It was already dead, having broken its neck in the collision. She laid the little creature on its back by the fireplace, and although the cats saw it there, not one made a move toward it. She explained that what cats like is the sport more than the victim or the eating. With the bird already dead there was no chase, no catch required, and the game had been ended.

The Bible speaks about the lion and the lamb sharing the same space as friends, but it has not happened yet, unless the lion is first hit with a tranquilizer. Sometimes the difference in size is huge, as with a mouse and an elephant.

Nevertheless, there is a hierarchy of fear that determines relationships in the animal kingdom, often within the same species. Friends of ours have goats—thirteen of them penned up in the backyard. When the goats have been fed and have time on their hands, they love to play king of the mountain. It goes on constantly, with the largest and larger goats pushing the smaller ones off the low sheds and feeding stations.

Life for many in the animal world boils down to the survival of the biggest as well as the fittest. It seems to be nature's way, creation's order. And we play a part in it. As noted in one other story in this book, animals eat each other, but humans eat animals also. It's just that when the "kill" is wrapped in cellophane and sold in a supermarket, it seems much more civilized than watching animals gorging themselves on other animals on TV. It's enough to make some folks vegetarians.

And no one will think me going too far to note that the survival of the biggest or the fittest is much the same in the human family. We not only often act like animals, but in the business world when mom and pop stores have to compete with Wal-Mart, Home Depot, and Lowes, size has a major part to play in the outcome. Governments speak of "negotiating from strength." And status is all over the place.

Are we like the animals, or are the animals like us? There is another kingdom, the kingdom of God which is to "come on earth, as it is in heaven," and when it does or as it does, there will be a humanness in humanity, a generosity of spirit, an acceptance of difference, and it will not take a war or the threat of one to bring about unity and oneness.

Conversation Starters

1. What for you was the funniest moment in this story?

2. Who was more surprised taking a cue from the pictures, the mice who saw the cat, or the cat who saw the dog?

3. Would we be so quick to eat animals if we had to kill them first?

4. If you liked this book you might like the sequel, *Chato and the Party Animals*. How are the two books similar?

A Single Chard

by Linda Sue Park

160 pages

(New York: Clarion Books, 2001)

> *A small village in Korea becomes known for pottery making,*
> *in part due to its soil. All potters compete for a royal com-*
> *mission. Min is a master potter whose secret helps him win,*
> *but not without the assistance of a lowly urchin.*

Tree-ear listens carefully to conversations in his town because a birth or death in a family affects the state of that household's garbage, which he checks regularly for leftover rice. His friend, Crane-man, likens him to a scrawny little tree, "noticed by none but hearing all." Actually, the name Tree-ear comes from the half-circled mushrooms that grow on dead or fallen tree trunks.

The place is Korea, the time period around A.D. 1200. They are an unlikely pair, living as they do beneath a bridge, Tree-ear an orphan and Crane-man who was born with only one leg. But the harshness of their existence has not blunted them to life's subtleties. For example, one day Tree-ear comes upon a man who is unwittingly marking a path with rice falling from his backpack. He wonders whether he should tell the man immediately or let more rice fall so he can pick it up for himself. Troubled by the ethics of this situation, he shares it with Crane-man. Crane-man first tells him it is good to puzzle over such questions—"It keeps one's mind sharp and off one's hunger." Then, he says, "Scholars read the great words of the world. But you and I must learn to read the world itself."

When Tree-ear gets a job working for Master Potter Kim, the boy's goal is to learn how to make beautiful vases, but his first assignment is just to cut wood for the kiln. There is one kiln in town and each potter takes a turn supplying the wood. Next he is sent to dig clay. As Tree-ear performs all his chores, never does Kim thank him, compliment him, or even explain any of his pottery techniques. He is cantankerous, perhaps because his only son has died, leaving him without an heir to whom he can pass on his secret.

Kim's wife, on the other hand, is the epitome of grace and kindness. When out of anger Tree-ear flings away his rice bowl, she says, "This bowl had a great desire to become my hat." From then on, Tree-ear eats only half the rice she gives him for lunch, intending to bring the rest back for Crane-man; yet at the end of each day he finds the bowl full.

The potter's village of Ch'ulp'o has become world famous in part because of its clay. It has just the right amount of iron to produce the exquisite gray-green color pottery known as celadon ware. Tree-ear also realizes that Kim's pottery is far superior to that of any other potter's. One day he discovers the secret while carrying out the task of draining the clay at the clay pit. The clay has to be screened for impediments and when glaze is needed, this process is completed five times before Kim accepts it. On that day while rubbing the clay for the fifth time Tree-Ear's fingers seem to tingle. He decides to do it two more times and that's it. That is what makes Kim's pottery so beautiful. The master potter never explains this, but Tree-ear discovers it. It has been there all the time; he had just not seen it before.

There is one reference to Buddhism in this story, but it comes across as something that is so much a part of the culture, it is taken for granted and is nothing special. However, there is a segment of

Buddhism known as Zen that reminds us of Tree-ear's suddenly seeing something that has been there all the time. In Zen this kind of happening occurs when one's mind is free and uncluttered. Then a Zen student can see a flower, for example, as if for the first time. One almost becomes that flower and views it from the inside with intense appreciation for its existence in the world.

The town is buzzing with excitement when the royal emissary for pottery comes to select the potter to receive the coveted commission from the emperor. It is a lifelong contract. (One of the unshared insights of this book is the value of art collectors. Though an elite segment of humanity, they provide others with work, self-esteem, and income.)

Kim works very hard for this award, but one aspect of the potter's work is unpredictable—the firing. The temperature in the kiln has to rise slowly for several days to prevent the clay from cracking or discoloring, and unbeknown to the potters at the time, other factors enter in causing trouble. Kim is a perfectionist, one who always throws away his first efforts, but on this occasion all the vases are discolored, so he smashes every one of them.

The emissary knows of Kim's work and visits him the next day to inform him that if he brings completed vases to the palace, his work will still be considered. Kim agrees to do this, but being an old man he knows he cannot walk the long distance to the palace. Tree-ear offers to be his legs.

Before Tree-ear departs, Crane-man offers sage advice. "Your mind knows you are going on a long journey, but you must not tell your body. It must think one hill, one valley, and one day at a time. In that way your spirit will not grow weary before you have even started." It sounds a bit like the aphorism, "a journey of a thousand miles begins with one step."

Crane-man also urges Tree-ear to visit the Rock of Falling Flowers along the way, a place at the top of a cliff. While he is there, thieves attack Tree-ear looking for rice. When they find only a pair of vases in his backpack, they become angry and throw them into the air. Tree-ear hears one of them smash to pieces on the rocks below. After the thieves leave, he searches the area where the vases landed and finds the first vase broken in a hundred pieces. The second vase is also broken but its larger shards stick in sand. He selects one shard and decides to continue on his journey to the palace and the royal emissary of pottery wares.

Tree-ear arrives there but being a lowly urchin he has trouble convincing the guard that he has a royal appointment. Finally he does, and has to tell the emissary that his vases were destroyed by thieves, but that he does have a single shard, about the size of his palm. It is enough. The emissary, who knows art well, sees what Master Potter Kim can do and grants him the commission.

The young apprentice is fed there and is given a trip home by boat, which is much easier. When he arrives at Kim's house and tells him about the commission, Kim shares some good news and some bad news. The bad news is that Crane-man had an accident and died. The good news I will leave to the readers to discover. The Newbery Award–winning story is a seamless weaving, and the end is a further reward for reading it.

Conversation Starters

1. Can you think of any other towns or cities that have become famous because of the natural elements that are located there or nearby?

2. What thoughts come to you when you think of someone who is as poor as Tree-ear and Crane-man being concerned not to steal food but to come by it honestly?

3. Does the story provide any hint as to why Kim was so lacking in kindness and grace?

4. What for you was the most memorable part of this story?

God's Care and Forgiveness

Shiloh

by Phyllis Reynolds Naylor

144 pages

(New York: Atheneum, 1991)

A boy and a dog sound like a sentimental relationship at best. However, when it cuts a swath through the meanness of the legal owner, poverty, and the Bible Belt, we hear overtones of understanding and forgiveness.

The overall theme of this Newbery book is the contrast between punishment and suffering love. A spin-off theme is that understanding and change come only from the second dynamic, not the first. The story begins when an eleven-year-old boy named Marty is attracted to a beagle that follows him home one day. When their eyes meet, it is as if a bond between them had been established before the world began. However, when the boy approaches the dog, the dog backs off, fear-ridden, prompting Marty to observe, "Something really hurts inside you when you see a dog cringe like that. You know somebody's been kicking at him. Beating on him, maybe." Marty names him Shiloh, a biblical word the author might have related to the "Messiah."

At first Marty's parents do not accept his enthusiasm for the dog. The civil law does not protect dogs from the cruelty of their owners. Besides, they reason, the world is full of dogs their owners mistreat. "You gotta get used to it, Marty!" Then, too, there may be another reason for their initial response. They are poor. They cannot afford to keep a dog. Thus, to feed it, Marty goes without food himself so as not to deprive the rest of the family of whatever is available. Love can call for sacrifice.

We encounter the evil in punishment when Marty and his father take the dog back to its owner, Judd. The dog trembles in fear at the sight of the trailer Judd lives in. Judd talks about kicking dogs when they do not obey. He responds to Shiloh having run away the way a parent might a naughty boy. He lets the dog see the other dogs eat their supper, but doesn't give Shiloh any—to teach him a lesson. Judd's "evil" streak emerges when we further learn that he cheats storeowners out of money, saying he gave a twenty-dollar bill when he gave only a ten. He also shoots deer out of season, even a female deer.

When the dog goes missing again, we see how morality can be affected by suffering love. Telling the truth is *the* moral issue for Marty's parents, more important than what happens to a dog, at least in the beginning. For Marty, telling the truth is not that simple. When Judd asks Marty to be on the lookout for the dog, Marty says he will, but to himself it's "a promise I wasn't going to keep, Jesus help me." On the other hand, his promise to protect Shiloh (before he brought him back to Judd) is one he will keep, "God strike me dead."

The story takes place in the southern region known as the "Bible Belt" or in this case rural West Virginia. In Marty's family the references to God and Jesus are used in a punitive way. For Marty's grandmother even the idea of a white lie conjures up punishment. Not only is hell a place where liars go, but she believes that if someone breaks a promise Jesus will make him blind. She is inclined to *use* Jesus as a warning and "she went to church Sunday morning and evening both." Marty and his grandmother represent a generation gap plus a gap in their perceptions of Jesus and Christianity.

For Marty, the "theology," or "Jesusology" as some call it, evolves in the direction of moral maturity. Does he return Shiloh once again or lie to protect the dog? Struggling with the issue, he finally formulates a prayer. "Jesus," he whispers, "which you want me to do? Be one hundred percent honest and carry that dog back to Judd so that one of your creatures can be kicked and starved all over again, or keep him here and fatten him up to glorify your creation?" It's a great question. How would *you* answer it? For Marty the question or prayer "seemed to answer itself," as if to suggest that the answer is already in his mind seeking to work itself through to his awareness.

Perhaps the deepest issue Marty confronts on his search for understanding occurs when he muses to himself, "Don't know if Shiloh's gettin' more human or I'm gettin' to be more dog. If Jesus ever comes back to earth again, I'm thinking, he'll come as a dog, because there isn't anything as humble or patient or loving or loyal as the dog I have in my arms right now."

One might be tempted to dwell on the idea that "dog" is "god" spelled backward, but that would be to miss a considerable amount of material in the book that lends meaning to Marty's observation. This material makes it sound as if Shiloh is Jesus when he was crucified. Over and over again Marty is amazed at how Shiloh does not bark. On one level it is as if he had the bark beaten out of him when he was a pup, and it just never came back, but on a deeper level it sounds like the silence with which Jesus responded to the blows of the soldiers or the taunts of King Herod on the occasion of Jesus' crucifixion. Whether the author intends to make this connection is not an issue here. If it was intended, then to talk about it is being true to the story. If it was unintended, to talk about it is still being true to the story. That's the way some stories are—they have overtones, and authors often say more than even they realize.

A poet from another century by the name of Francis Thompson likened Jesus to a dog when he entitled his poem, "The

Hound of Heaven." Thompson saw God at work in Jesus, not letting us go, but always seeking to show his love and mercy. Shiloh and Marty do this in relation to each other. Each becomes an extension of the other so that it is hard to tell who is dog and who is human. There are many animal lovers who would understand this, knowing how their pets at times display "human" qualities.

All of the major characters struggle with moral development. The parents struggle with what is the right thing to do. At first the father goes by the letter of the law. The dog legally belongs to Judd and that's all there is to it. If he mistreats his dogs, there is nothing anyone can do about it, because that is his privilege by right of ownership. The father and mother, however, wrestle with a higher law, and this represents the need to keep civil laws fair and just. As Martin Luther King Jr. once put it, "An unjust law is no law at all."

Even Judd is presented as a person who can change. Also in relation to him, we see a hint of understanding in the form of compassion coming from the author. Judd has a reason for being mean and is not totally satisfied with being that way. He admits to Marty on one occasion that as a boy his father beat him so badly that he could barely put on his shirt, and at that moment Marty feels a twinge of pity for him. In other words, Judd is mean because he never experienced kindness during his formative years.

The real hope for Judd or potential for change comes when he confronts the suffering love of Marty in relation to Shiloh. Marty decides to go to Judd's trailer and offer to buy the dog. On the way a shot rings out and a deer falls. Judd steps out of the woods, shouting that he got himself a deer. When he sees Marty, he steps back because it isn't deer season, and the one he killed was a doe.

Marty uses what he sees to keep Shiloh. He offers to keep quiet about what he saw if Judd gives him the dog. Judd agrees but only if Marty promises to work for him for twenty hours to pay an additional amount. Marty goes along with it and insists that Judd write this on a piece of paper and sign it, unusual fore-sight for one so young. However, when he shows up for work Judd proceeds to overwork him, taking his meanness out on the eleven-year-old boy. While Marty labors splitting wood in the hot sun Judd sips a beer, and on the first day or two he doesn't even offer Marty a drink of water. Then on the third day Judd laughs, saying the piece of paper is worthless since there is no witness. Although this saddens Marty, he keeps his side of the bargain and works even harder, a response that perplexes Judd. He begins to soften just a bit; he offers Marty some water.

They talk more about Judd's background. Judd had earlier revealed his view of dogs by not even giving them names. However, at one point in that conversation he refers to Marty's dog as Shiloh, implying that this, too, was not lost on him.

I am not going to divulge the way this story ends and even if I did, that would not end it, because *Shiloh* became the first of a trilogy about the dog, Marty, and Judd. The other two, *Shiloh Season* and *Saving Shiloh*, continue the story. This book, how-ever, is a great introduction to the series. It is realistic. It is true to the ongoing struggle between good and evil that is in all of us. It reveals the degree to which religion can be distorted, and it has overtones of forgiveness and moral and spiritual growth.

Conversation Starters

1. Why should Marty (or anybody) have to get used to the presence of evil in the world?

2. Do you own a dog? If you do, how would you describe the relationship?

3. Is it always best to tell the truth?

4. What makes many dogs long-suffering, humble, and loyal?

Bud, Not Buddy

by Christopher Paul Curtis

256 pages

(New York: Delacorte Press, 1999)

> *Hope is a four-letter word that seems to follow a ten-year-old orphan around as he looks for his father. He doesn't use the word* hope, *but looking back on his journey it comes through at some crucial times.*

An upbeat theme is even tied to the boy's name—Bud. His mother gives it to him and has in mind the way buds on flowers are just waiting to spring to life and add beauty to the scenery. That's why "Buddy" is not enough (it sounds like the name of a dog). Of course, Bud never tells anybody his mother's flowery thoughts, but he never misses the chance to tell someone his name is "Bud, not Buddy," the title of this Newbery book.

One form hope takes in this story is that when some doors close, another seems to open. Alone and hungry in Flint, Michigan, Bud follows his stomach to a downtown mission that serves meals. Times are hard and "bread lines" are common. He turns the corner only to find a lot of other hungry people in front of him. Moreover, they stop serving breakfast at 7:00 A.M. He is already late and about to leave when a man looks down at him and says, "Clarence, what took you so long? Get back in line with your momma." And before he can tell them his real name, he is now the newest member of a family of four. Since the man is big, nobody dares challenge him and Bud gets some breakfast.

There were many people in food lines then. The shadow of the Great Depression still lingers, all of which makes a sign that hangs on the outside wall of the building, just above the line, seem out of place. It shows a well-dressed white family in a large car, each one dressed to the nines, and around the edge of the sign are the words, THERE'S NO PLACE LIKE AMERICA TODAY. Presumably the words relate to the family in the car, not to the people on the sidewalk waiting for a meal. Still, there are many folks who feel that way about America today. They aren't the ones who are hungry, and those that are don't dare say otherwise, lest someone think they are unpatriotic or chronic complainers.

The reason Bud is looking for a place to eat is that he has just escaped from his third foster home. "Escaped" is a fair word because the Amos family is worse than the orphanage, no thanks to their son Todd. Bigger than Bud, he is in the process of beating him up when the bedroom door opens and Todd's mother stands there. Suddenly Todd acts like the victim. He pretends he is having another asthma attack, this one brought on by Bud picking on him. It is an example of blaming the victim. In any event, Bud is to spend the night in a dirty, dark shed out back, before being sent back to the orphanage. During the night he decides it is time to get out of there, and with some hornets providing extra incentive, he does.

Meeting up with a friend from the Home, they decide to jump a train, but Bud can't run fast enough and his friend, realizing this, tosses Bud his suitcase that he guards with his life. In it is an old blanket, some flyers that tell about his father, and some rocks with strange writing on them. He keeps them because they are from his mother who has died, and because he thinks the rocks might be important.

Bud sets out walking to Grand Rapids, where he knows his father lives. Reaching the city limits of Flint a sign says "You are

41

now leaving Flint, hurry back." The other side of the sign reads, "Welcome to Flint," so for a few minutes he has fun jumping in and out of Flint.

With night not far off, Bud gets a little scared when a car slows down and stops. He hides in the woods but the driver, a Mr. Lewis, coaxes him out. He, too, is African American and knows that walking alone on a highway is not a safe thing to do. He is going back to Grand Rapids the next morning so he gives Bud a ride. He also has a sense of humor. Mr. Lewis sees how skinny Bud is and says it's a good thing Bud's legs don't touch when he walks "'cause if those two twigs got to rubbing against one another he'd have a fire going in no time."

When Bud tells Mr. Lewis his father's name is Herman Calloway, Mr. Lewis informs Bud that everybody knows who Herman Calloway is—a bandleader. In Grand Rapids Bud persuades Mr. Lewis to drop him off where his father's band is known to rehearse without telling Mr. Lewis he has never met his father. Bud walks into the building and sees a group of men on a stage sitting in a circle, talking. One of them is white. Racism was strong in Michigan back in the 1930s and one example is that it is against the law for an African American to own any property so the place where they rehearse is in the white man's name.

The one Bud assumes is his "father" has his back to him but Bud hears him tell about a man that is so old "he could have been a waiter at the Last Supper." When Bud sees his father's face he is shocked because he, too, is very old, at least to a young ten-year-old's eyes. The waiter at the Last Supper must have had some help.

Bud's "father" does not recognize him when Bud says he has come to meet him. All eyes look to the drummer, but Bud looks at old Herman and says, "I know it's you."

The band members respond to this and take Bud to dinner in a restaurant, the first restaurant food Bud has ever had. It amazes Bud that each member of the band has something different to eat from a menu. He's never seen a menu before. There Bud meets Miss Thomas, the band's singer, and at a house later she shows him the room in which he will sleep. He learns it was once a little girl's room, but now she is gone.

The band sort of adopts Bud. They give him a fancy musician's name, "Sleepy La Bone," which comes from his sleeping late one morning and his being so skinny. They also give him a recorder so he can begin to learn music. He has to help with the chores of the band, but he loves every minute of it. Compared with life in the Home, it is all a pleasure, and when Miss Thomas tells Bud, "You're home now," they are the sweetest words he has heard in a long time, maybe ever.

The elderly Herman Calloway is having a hard time accepting Bud as a member of the band. He thinks of him as a con artist out to worm some money out of him. The old man comes across to Bud as a person with edges that one had to be careful about. At first it is like one of those closing doors, but as previously in Bud's young life, it led to another one opening. The details of this are worth the price of admission, as the saying goes, but I do want to leave the reader with a couple of hints to stir up the curiosity.

One is that Herman Calloway is gruff. It's not just the way a young man happens to perceive him. And there is a reason for it. Not too many years ago, Herman had a daughter whom he hoped would go to college. She would be the first one in his family to do this, so he was protective of her. He was strict with her, too strict. She rebelled and ran off with one of his drummers, and Herman has never seen her again. The memory hangs like a weight on his heart, and does not go away.

The second hint occurs after the band plays a concert some distance from Grand Rapids. Mr. C. is outside kicking some stones with his foot. When he finds the one he wants, he asks Bud to pick it up for him, because he is getting too old to bend down. Bud hands it to him and after Herman writes something on it, he then adds it to a bunch of stones in the glove compartment of his car. Bud sees there is writing on them and says, "I've got some of those too," and he shows him.

At first Mr. C. accuses Bud of stealing them from a drawer in his room, but Bud tells him he had got them from his mother, and if you are giving this a little thought you will not be surprised to learn that Bud's mother and Herman Calloway are related. She is his daughter and that makes Bud his grandson. How Herman comes to believe this has a lot to do with the rocks that Bud shows him, and the writing on each of them. However, these hints are like clues to a mystery, the mystery of how roots in this case grew out of the rocks.

Conversation Starters

1. Why was the suitcase so important to Bud?

2. Why did Herman cry?

3. What part does humor play in this story?

4. How do you feel about a new door opening up when a prior one seems to close? It is always true?

Wemberly Worried

by Kevin Henkes

32 pages

(New York: Greenwillow Books, 2000)

> *Wemberly worried about everything. Big things, little things, and things in between. When it was time for school to start, she worried even more. But something happened at school that changed her mind.*

In these post-September 11 times, worrying has become a contagious disease that many people have caught, or it has caught them. The odds of someone contracting anthrax, for example, are one in twenty million, and because it is treatable, the odds of dying from it are one in seventy million. And yet we worry.

The worries of Wemberly the mouse seem tame by comparison, but to her they are big. Soaking in a hot bath, she worries she might shrink. She worries that the tree in her front yard might fall on her house. (It stood as straight as a phone pole.) Sitting in her living room, she worries that the crack in the wall might widen and something might come out of it. Her family tries to assure her, but their litany of "You worry too much" are just words with no effect. They are like authorities telling her she *should* not be that way, when it is the only way she knows how to be. By insisting that she not worry, they are not accepting her or her worries as a part of her.

When Wemberly must start school, her worries become larger. On her list are a bunch of "what if's": "What if no else has spots?...What if the teacher is mean? What if the room smells bad?...What if I can't find the bathroom? What if I hate the snack? What if I have to cry?"

What changes things for Wemberly is meeting another girl at school—Jewel—who also brings a doll with her, stands alone all by herself, and also has spots, of all things. For Wemberly, it's like looking in a mirror. She experiences acceptance. Her worries dissolve when she meets someone who is just like she is.

When my daughter graduated from college, the dean met with the graduates and their parents. She said that if there was any wish she had for the class, it was that throughout their lives they would always have at least one good friend. By friend she meant a Jewel, someone with whom a person could be himself or herself.

It is a bit amazing that such a simple story can convey such depth and content, for what is really going on here is very spiritual. It gets to the heart of the Christian faith whether or not the author is aware of it. On one level, the story is about the difference between law and grace. Wemberly's family is the law, telling her what she ought to do or be, whereas her new friend is unconditional grace for her. She is a jewel and not in name only. She is a way of giving Wemberly acceptance, full and complete, the kind God gives. On another level, the story also shows a way to move outside fear. Because Wemberly understands only too well the fears that Jewel is suffering, Wemberly reaches outside herself to another; and in comforting another, her own worries seem smaller.

Conversation Starters

1. Do you have any worries or fears? Can you say why?

2. Does anyone in your family have worries?

3. If so, reflecting on them, what responses do they bring from members of the family?

4. What do you think about the effect Jewel and Wemberly had on each other?

Preacher's Boy

by Katherine Paterson

160 pages

(New York: Clarion Books, 1999)

> *With the end of the world just six months off, according to some, Robbie, a preacher's kid, decides he's going to work everything in while there is time. To do this means for him no longer believing in God, which he mistakenly assumes he can just shut off like the dial on a radio.*

My husband and I are preacher's kids, as is Newbery Award–winning author Katherine Paterson (though for other titles). So I looked forward to reading this, with my own childhood and adolescent memories still in mind. It's a funny book, with great language and great ideas.

The time and setting are Vermont, summer of 1899. Robbie, the preacher's kid, feels the whole town is watching his every move to make sure he is "clean and good." Robbie's dad is not allowed to be himself either. He is too easy on sin and not thrilled enough about eternal damnation, some parishioners say. He does say that war is hell, but that isn't the hell some parish pillars have in mind.

Parishioners got their view of religion from the preacher's predecessor, Rev. Pelkam. Robbie's father feels he spent twelve years "mopping up the damage" from Pelkam's sermons. Pelkam was a good man, according to Robbie's dad, but afraid of new ideas, like those on evolution from Charles Darwin.

The troubles begin when Robbie and his friend run Mabel Cramm's bloomers up the town flagpole. When the church deacon sees the bloomers on the flagpole, he concludes it is a symbol of the moral decay that is rotting America. Perhaps it would help to invite Rev. Pelkam back for a pulpit visit, which the church does. Pelkam stays in the manse and after a second helping of griddlecakes he is ready to tell the world not to trust temporal things. He rails against smoking and drinking, impure thoughts and bad language. He invites parishioners to repent and join him in sitting at table in the Eternal Kingdom of Righteousness. For Robbie the prospects of sitting across from him forever are daunting.

While Robbie is glad to have his dad for a father, the fear Rev. Pelkam promotes causes Robbie to decide to convert to "apeism" (a link with evolution), as his friend calls it. The term *atheism* has not yet become a household word. Also influencing his thinking is the fear that many religious people had at the time—that the world would end in January 1900. If so, there are many things Robbie wants to do before then, and not believing in God anymore would make it easier to do them. True, it might wreck his plans for the future, but he wouldn't have to think about sin because the Ten Commandments would no longer apply to him. He has not heard of the idea that if there were no commandments we would have to invent some anyway to function as a society.

With these questions burning in his brain, Robbie decides he needs some time to think, so he travels to an abandoned cabin in the woods—which only he and his friend know about—but as he draws near someone is already inside, snoring loudly. The cabin is falling apart, and the snorer, an older man, isn't exactly in good shape either. He smells terrible. A young daughter has accompanied the older man and she lives up to her name, Vile, which is short for Violet. They are dirt poor, out of food, and in need of a roof above them. Though no longer a believer, Robbie remembers that God wants us to be kind and helpful to others, and the two squatters become his social ministry project. "I might be an apeist who didn't have to obey the commandments, but that didn't mean I had lost all human feeling."

A memorable moment in the story occurs as Robbie and his friend, Willie, go for a swim. When two other boys steal their clothes, Robbie swims out to them and almost drowns one of them. His feelings had been building ever since the boys poked fun at Robbie's brother, Elliot, who is mentally disabled.

Willie intervenes. Robbie swears he would never have actually drowned the boy, but he knows deep down that he has quite a temper and did feel like doing it. This moment in the story is a classic example of why neither the Fifth Commandment nor capital punishment deters murder. For deterrence to be effective a person would have to think about the consequence in advance, but 95 percent of homicides are crimes of impulse or passion. Such persons are filled with rage, not rational thought. Robbie feels the anger but it isn't until he simmers down that he feels badly about it.

Vile and her father, Jeb, are penniless, but Jeb still manages to get some medicinal alcohol to dull the pain of living. Robbie shares a plan with Vile about getting some money by writing in a note that Robbie had been kidnapped, but the scheme falls apart when Vile throws away the medicinal alcohol her father, Jeb, was drinking, and he becomes violent about it. He finds the note, stuffs it into his pocket, and storms down the hill into town to invade a pharmacy and get some more booze.

When Jeb is arrested, the police find the note and assume he killed Robbie after kidnapping him. His trial is to be in a nearby town. Robbie shows up at the trial, mindful of telling the truth and not bearing false witness (another commandment he could not get out of his head). Jeb is freed and allowed to go with his daughter under the watchful eye of Robbie's father.

I will not divulge the ending, other than to say it is an appropriate one. The book is a good read and provides an insight into what it was like to be a preacher's kid at the beginning of the twentieth century. The response of Robbie to the poverty of Jeb and Vile is the timeless part, and the religious landscape is still littered with preacher's kids who have reacted differently to life in glass houses. Even the turn-of-the-century fears have been mirrored in our own fears of the Y2K bug and other millennium disasters.

Conversation Starters

1. Was Robbie a genuine atheist? If not, why not?

2. Why do you think some children and adolescents go through a time when church and religion are a turnoff for them?

3. Why do some people get more fearful about the end of the world than others?

Mrs. Katz and Tush

by Patricia Polacco

32 pages

(New York: Dell, 1992)

> *A kitten becomes the means whereby an elderly, lonely Jewish woman and a young African American boy become friends. Getting to know each other reveals how much they have in common. The relationship makes them members of the same family.*

A woman of color stops by each day to see an old lady, Mrs. Katz, who is alone and seemingly friendless. The woman brings her son along who offers Mrs. Katz the last kitten their cat had, which no one wants because it is the runt of the litter. The old lady agrees to accept it, providing the boy, Larnel, will help her take care of it. Since it has no tail, they name it Tush, because that's all one sees when viewing that part of the kitten's anatomy. Mrs. Katz watches the kitten play and observes, "Such a person."

Mrs. Katz is from Warsaw, Poland, and as she and the boy begin to get acquainted, she reminds him that they both came from slavery. It is a bond, her side beginning in Egypt and his in America. Larnel realizes that since she is Jewish, she is not allowed to go to certain places here in America. It is easy to assume that America is a land of liberty and justice for all, but that is not always true. When Mrs. Katz watches Larnel she can only think, "Such a person."

Their friendship unfolds when Mrs. Katz invites Larnel to share a Seder with her. It is both a sad and happy occasion, bringing to mind, she informs her young friend, all the people who "suffered so we could be free." It is appropriate to digress for a moment with the word *free*. In the Boston area there is a train station called Back Bay. At the top of a long escalator passengers enter the street level of the terminal and directly in front of them is a life-sized statue of A. Philip Randolph, founder of the Brotherhood of Sleeping Car Porters here in America. His words are chiseled into the base of the stone: "Freedom is never a final fact, but a continuing evolutionary process to higher and higher levels of human social, economic, political, and religious relationships."

In a practical way freedom is a lull between storms, or a moment of respite between problems. On a personal, physical level, something like chronic pain can visit us for a long time, without giving us any freedom. This is also true of addictions, poverty, tempers, and a host of other human baggage. Other sources of trouble seem built into society, namely, greed, lust, and pride. They never seem to go away, and then in the midst of these itches we have hate, anger, and envy. Freedom is not a fait accompli but a process in which we are always participating with other people on Earth as Mr. Randolph so wisely stated.

Mrs. Katz and Tush ends with memorable scenes of Mrs. Katz along with Larnel and one of his own children. There are graduations, weddings, and new babies to experience together— and even a kaddish, a funeral prayer. The book ends with the following words:

> Larnel stood in front of the headstone.
> He read from her book.
> He placed a small rock on top of her headstone.

Then he, his wife, and their children read the inscription together.

MRS. KATZ, OUR BUBEE…SUCH A PERSON.

Conversation Starters

1. Some friendships last, some do not. Why is that?

2. What for you is most important in a friendship?

3. What is the meaning of the phrase, "Such a person?"

4. In what way does this story show us how people of different backgrounds can be friends?

Justice for All

Tar Beach

by Faith Ringgold

32 pages

(New York: Crown, 1991)

> *Looking at the stars can make one feel rather small. To Cassie they are an invitation to do anything she wants to do, such as fly. She entertains her thoughts as if they were honored guests.*

Our daughter is a commercial airline pilot and one reason she loves to fly at night is having such a view of the stars. Another is the freedom she feels way up there. An unspoken factor is that all the troubles of the world are left behind, though she acknowledges that terrorists using airplanes do enter her thoughts on occasion.

Describing the roof of a building coated with a layer of tar as "Tar Beach" is a fitting description, especially if getting to a real beach is not that easy to do. The tar beach in this picture book launches Cassie Louise Lightfoot into flights of fancy. Nowhere in the text does author/illustrator Faith Ringgold use the word *dream*, but she writes how "sleeping on Tar Beach was magical." Whether through dream or pure imagination, from the tar beach Cassie is transported above various locations in New York City.

When Cassie sees the stars above her, they provide a lift to her mind and spirit. Many of us have had that experience. True, it can be a humbling moment, but it is also awesome. Cassie is not only awed by the stars but also by the sights she sees when she flies around the city. Dreams can take us anywhere, but for Cassie certain special places fill her mind.

One of those special places is above the George Washington Bridge, which she can see from her rooftop. What makes it special is that her father helped build the bridge and it was opened on her birthday in 1931. That makes it a kind of unspoken birthday present, one she did not learn about until she got older. Tied in with this view of things is the feeling that whatever she sees from her bird's-eye view she owns.

Indeed, the power of ownership is a key motif in this story. It takes on an edge of poignancy when Cassie flies over the Union Building. It houses the union that oversees the workers on the skyscraper and those who worked on the bridge-building project. Cassie's father is also helping to build the Union Building. Although he walks on steel girders and is called the Cat, he is not allowed to join the union of the company that hires him, not even to work on their building. The reason? It's something called a "grandfather clause," an infamous bit of red tape that prevented many African American workers from becoming union members. The ruling stated that if someone's father did not belong to the union, his son or any member of the family is likewise excluded. Injustice is written all over it like red pencil markings on a test, but it was in force for decades.

When Cassie flies over the Union Building and takes ownership, it allows her to give the building to her father, which of course means that, since he owns the building, he does not have to join the union. Several other benefits come from his ownership, one being that he will not have to look for work during the winter months. Structural steel work is dangerous at any time of the year, but when the girders are covered with ice it is impossible, so nonunionized laborers are laid off and have to find other work for themselves. This makes Cassie's mother cry.

Another benefit from owning these buildings is that having money allows Cassie and her family to enjoy the pleasures the wealthy white population takes for granted, such as sleeping late in the morning and having ice cream whenever they want it.

Cassie tells her brother Be Be that it is easy to fly. One just needs somewhere to go that "you can't get to any other way." Ms. Ringgold observes in her one-page commentary that flying was a common method of wish fulfillment for slaves. It reminded me of a song—"If I had the wings of an angel, over these prison walls I would fly." One can understand how fitting it would be for inmates in a prison to be able to fly, but that many Americans who live outside of prison are nonetheless living behind walls of a different sort is a sad commentary.

Many African Americans have joined the middle and upper classes, but there are many of them, and poor people of all colors, who can still only reach these goals in their imagination. It is as if the only way to truly live is to live in a dream world.

Ms. Ringgold has another book that begins with the idea of flying. It was published one year after *Tar Beach* under the title *Aunt Harriet's Underground Railroad in the Sky*. It, too, is a story about Cassie and her brother, but whereas they begin their sojourn by flying, most of it is spent very much down to earth repeating the oftentimes harrowing experiences of slaves attempting to flee slavery by way of the underground railroad. It is an excellent resource on these experiences.

A word or two should be said about the beautiful story quilt that is shown at the end of the book. The quilt now hangs in the Guggenheim Museum in New York City. Readers can revel in its beauty as each page of the book has some of the colorful quilt blocks decorating the page borders.

Conversation Starters

1. Can you think of any places that you can only get to by dreaming about them or imagining them?

2. Should dreaming about something one wants be discouraging or encouraging?

3. What do you think it might be like to be an African American in earlier times and see all the advantages most white Americans have, but be unable to have them for oneself?

Martin's Big Words

by Doreen Rappaport

illustrated by Bryan Collier

40 pages

(New York: Hyperion, 2001)

> *In this Caldecott Honor book about the life of Martin Luther King Jr., a few of his words, plus some from the author, and pictures serve as prompters to call forth feelings in the reader.*

"Big words" are often interpreted as words that are long or difficult to understand, but that is not what one finds in this book, so the phrase must mean something else. On an introductory page, the illustrator encourages each reader to "bring his or her experience to it." Once I was transported into the book with the aid of the wonderful watercolor and cut paper collage artwork, the title started to speak a different language.

For example, one pair of Martin's big words are "hate" and "love." They are linked with the idea that "hate cannot drive out hate, only love can do that." The logic of this said to me that hate is like a fire that only water (love) can put out.

"Together" and "separate" are another pair of Martin's big words. They relate to hate and love. Hate separates, but love unites. It removes barriers, but often the way this works is like surgery. On one of the pages the words note how white

61

southerners "hated and feared Martin's big words." When he backed up nonviolent action with love, there was nothing they could do to stop the effect it had on them and on other people. It brought out the hatred that causes separation, which they knew deep down. His words and deeds were the handwriting on the walls of their hearts and their violent responses burned themselves out.

Martin believed this was "God's movement" and thus it could not be stopped. The white response of jailing, beating, and killing African Americans had only a human spirit in it, not God's, and so it died. White southerners lost the will to kill, and when that happened, the internal war within them came to an end. At least this is what the words "God's movement" said to me.

The action that carried the love to white hearts and minds in the South begins when Rosa Parks refuses to yield her seat on a bus to a white man who demands it. The law that forced African Americans to sit in the back was not written down but was a part of the culture of the South. This led to a boycott of the bus system in Montgomery that lasted 381 days. A picture in the book shows an empty bus being driven on a street. Another shows a young African American man looking at a row of buses parked in the bus companies' lot. It was a kind of surgery on the white capitalistic soul, but it worked and helped heal an old wound.

White clergy and city officials counseled Martin to wait, to not act rashly, but he replied that they had been waiting 340 years and if nothing was done they would be waiting another 340 years. The time had come to act.

One of the first pictures that greets the reader's eyes shows an African American youth pointing to a sign that reads, "White Only." After just ten years of Martin's nonviolent approach to violence, those signs came down without African American citizens firing a shot. It was similar to the way Mahatma Gandhi's nonviolent response brought an end to British oppression.

"Peace" and "war" are another pair of Martin's big words. They brought to my mind his protest against the war in Vietnam, and the nonviolent response of American students to that war. They also relate to our war on terrorism. Martin's big words are still "alive for us today," as the last page of the text part informs us.

Part of Martin's well-known "I Have a Dream" speech is quoted in the book. The part about African American and white boys and girls walking hand in hand brought to mind a Martin Luther King Jr. breakfast I attended at Bridgewater State College in honor of his birthday. African Americans and whites attended the breakfast, sat at the same tables, and ended the two-hour celebration singing "We Shall Overcome." We stood in one large circle of 500 people and held hands. When Martin first referred to boys and girls, parent readers might have been of that age. But we are older now and we are still holding hands on such an occasion. It is a good sign, a promise of hope.

In 1964 Martin Luther King Jr. received the Nobel prize for peace. The illustration shows a little African American girl's face against a background of the American flag, somewhat tattered and torn, perhaps due to war. There is something extremely offensive about large white policemen hitting young African American girls with their nightsticks, and I could not help but wonder how African Americans could respond peacefully. It would have been hard for me to do so as a white American.

One of the final illustrations shows four candles in a church with Martin looking in through the window. Each candle represents one of the four young girls whose lives ended in a Birmingham, Alabama, church when a bomb was thrown into it by white men.

For me perhaps the most powerful set of words in the book mentions Martin's death. He had gone to Memphis, Tennessee, to help garbage workers strike for fair wages. On the first day he walked, talked, sang, and prayed with them. On the second day he was shot, and he died. That was April 4, 1968, and with that bullet the life of a great American came to an end but not its influence, as this book reveals.

The book concludes with a list of "Important Dates" in the life of Martin Luther King Jr. as well as a list of additional books and web sites. Take time to look at them to see which ones you'd like to pursue.

Conversation Starters

1. Revenge is a powerful human emotion. How did Martin cool it off?

2. What for you was the most powerful set of words in this book?

3. What was the most powerful illustration?

4. What do you usually do on the holiday honoring the birthday of Martin Luther King Jr.?

Number the Stars

by Lois Lowry

144 pages

(New York: Dell, 1989)

> *Germany's guns and tanks were no match for the wit and courage of Danish citizens, personalized in this story about a ten-year-old girl by the name of Annemarie Johansen and her friend, Ellen Rosen.*

"Who is that man who rides past here every morning on his horse?" a German soldier asked a young Danish lad.

"He is the king of Denmark," the boy replied.

"Where is his bodyguard?" the soldier asked.

"All of Denmark is his bodyguard," the boy replied.

The loyalty implicit in that historic question and answer is in dramatic contrast to the well-known atmosphere in Germany where, surrounded by soldiers, Hitler was subjected to plots by its citizens to assassinate him. Equally well known was the risk involved in befriending German Jews. No one knew which neighbor might inform the police of such a gesture.

In Denmark, on the other hand, there was a national response to smuggle Danish Jews out of the country under the noses of German soldiers. Gentile neighbors looked after their vacated houses, watered plants, dusted furniture, and polished candlesticks. Although it is speculative, it is easy to wonder if the name of the Danish king and his daily ride through Copenhagen had something to do with it. His last name was Christian, and at least his name and his ride kept that word on the minds of the people. Perhaps it even moved them to action in keeping with that word. This is a story of one family and their daughter who demonstrated that spirit whether they were aware of its source or not.

This spirit takes hold on the evening of the Jewish New Year in 1943. As the members of the Jewish congregation listen to their rabbi, he warns them that German occupation forces are going to "relocate" all Jewish citizens. A high-ranking German official named G. F. Duchwitz informed the rabbi of this. He is identified at the end of the book where the author indicates elements of the story that are historically true. Those who heeded the warning left the city quickly or went into hiding.

Gentile Christians in Denmark pick up this announcement and begin to hide their Jewish friends. One family that does this is named Johansen. Their daughter, Annemarie, and Ellen Rosen, a Jewish girl, are best friends, and most of the story weaves their relationship into the response to the German occupation. That night Ellen comes to stay at Annemarie's house and assumes the identity of Annemarie's older sister, Lise, who had been killed in a car accident two weeks before her wedding.

German officials knock on the Johansen door during the night and insist on searching for the Rosens whom they have learned might be hiding there. They do not find them but then they approach the door to the room of Annemarie, who has been listening at the door. Ellen quickly tries to undo the clasp of the Jewish Star of David necklace that hangs from her neck. Annemarie yanks it off just as the officials enter her room. She presses the star into her hand so hard that when the soldiers subsequently leave, the imprint is embedded in her palm. Exciting details like this will keep a reader turning the pages, even though the war may seem like ancient history.

A conversation with Annemarie's fisherman uncle leads to the two girls and Mrs. Johansen departing by train for his town on the seacoast. Upon arrival they learn that a casket will be brought to the uncle's house because a Great-aunt Birte has died, and it is the custom in Denmark to sit with the body. Annemarie did not even know she had a Great-aunt Birte and becomes suspicious that something is afoot. A small number of people come to the house that night along with some German officers who say they have seen people coming and wonder what is going on. When they are told about the death in the family, the officer insists on them opening the casket until Mrs. Johansen calmly tells him that the great-aunt died of typhus, but they would be willing to open the casket for one last look.

"Typhus" is the magic word and the officer and his men quickly leave the house. When the casket is later opened, it is discovered to contain warm clothing and blankets to be used by the Rosens and perhaps some of the others there that night who are hoping to escape to Sweden in Uncle Henrik's fishing boat. Before leaving for the boat, a psalm is read containing the words "Number the stars" from which the title of the book comes. In this case it refers to the large number of Jewish people who escaped from Denmark, close to 7,000. It also brings to my mind the Jewish Children's Memorial in Jerusalem, which is a part of Yad Vashem—the world's foremost Holocaust memorial and museum whose name comes from Isaiah and means "an everlasting memorial." One part of the museum is in total darkness except for the simulation of stars in the ceiling. As one walks through this area using guide rails, a recorded narrator intones the names, ages, and countries of origin of all the children killed in the concentration camps. The effect is most sobering.

Ellen Rosen is fortunate. She and her parents escape that night in a Danish fishing boat, but not without continued support from their friends, including a special effort by Annemarie.

Mr. Rosen is given an envelope to bring with him to the boat, but he drops it outside the house. It is absolutely imperative that Uncle Henrik be given this envelope. When it is discovered on the doorstep, it becomes Annemarie's task to carry it to the boat in the dead of night. Her mother places it at the bottom of a basket containing Uncle Henrik's lunch so the girl can tell anyone who stops her that he forgot his lunch.

German soldiers, holding snarling dogs on leashes, do stop her. The soldiers eat the bread and some cheese and then discover the envelope. When a soldier opens it he throws it on the ground because it contains an embroidered handkerchief he has no use for. They let Annemarie go. She retrieves the envelope and its contents, and brings it to her uncle.

Later in the fact pages at the end of the book, the importance of the handkerchief is explained. Many Danish fishing boats participated in smuggling Danish Jews to Sweden. It became essential for every fishing captain to have one of these handkerchiefs because the Germans had discovered Jews in hidden compartments in a couple of boats. The Danes threw rotting fish on the decks, but the Germans brought trained dogs who could sniff out human bodies despite the fish odor. Then some Swedish scientists came up with a mixture of dried rabbit's blood and cocaine, which was applied to the cloth. When soldiers came on board, the captain, faking a cold, would drop the handkerchief. The dogs would immediately go to the scent of the rabbit but when they sniffed the cocaine it temporarily deadened their sense of smell, so they could not detect any human beings hiding on the boat. It was a ruse that worked, and the Germans never figured out how so many Jews escaped from Denmark.

Conversation Starters

1. What moments of courage do you find in the book?

2. How would you compare this story with the *Diary of Anne Frank?*

3. What do you think of the possible influence of the Danish king's name and his daily ride through the streets of the nation's capital?

Amazing Grace

by Mary Hoffman

illustrated by Caroline Binch

32 pages

(New York: Dial Books, 1991)

> *"Amazing" is an adjective describing a girl named Grace. It also describes the origin of that term. The power in the origin comes through to Grace whether or not the author had that origin in mind.*

Some time ago at a rock concert in New York featuring the group Guns and Roses, the crowd responded to the loud sound system music with enthusiasm. When the concert ended, the band left the stage and Jessie Norman, the opera star, walked out alone and began singing "Amazing grace, how sweet the sound that saved a wretch like me." With the first stanza the crowd grew quiet. With the second, you could hear a pin drop, and with the third stanza some began singing along with her.

When a group of adults were asked why this happened, one person said, "It is America's hymn," and another said, "Everyone can identify with what it means to feel wretched, and grace is a word of hope."

Upon seeing the title to this book many readers will think of the hymn that bears the same name. They may have bought it expecting to see some reference to it, but there is none. Not one! At first it looks as if the writer used the title to sell the book. However, readers are in for a pleasant surprise.

In this story, Grace is the name of a girl, and she is amazing because of her ability to see herself as the person she reads about or hears about. Many children have imaginations, even vivid ones, but Grace's carries her further. She is moved by her imagination to act out the lead person in the story. Thus, when her grandmother reads to her about Joan of Arc, Grace uses the lid of a garbage can as a shield, holds up a make-believe sword, and calls her troops to follow her into a make-believe battle.

When she hears about Hiawatha, the Native American chief of the famous poem, she puts on a headdress and sits cross-legged on a rug with her arms folded in front of her. When the story is about the Trojan Horse, she makes a horse out of a cardboard box, hangs a pillow on a broomstick for its head, and hides inside like a soldier waiting to surprise the citizens of Troy. She sees herself a man or a woman with equal ease.

The purpose of this book is to show that Grace, a young African American girl, can be anything she sets her mind to being. Then one day this desire and determination surfaces in her classroom at school, not just in the safe confines of her home. The teacher announces they will do the play *Peter Pan* and there is no doubt in Grace's mind who she would like to be.

The public school world, however, is different from her home and no sooner has she expressed her desire to be Peter Pan then one of her classmates, Raj, says, "You can't be Peter—that's a boy's name." Her friend, Natalie, follows this up with a whisper in her ear, "You can't be Peter Pan. He isn't black."

The comment makes Grace feel sad and her mother angry, but her grandmother had a different response to the racial remark. Nana smiles and assures Grace that she can be anything she wants if she puts her mind to it. The next day Nana takes Grace downtown to a theater where the ballet *Romeo and Juliet* is being performed. They go to the front of the theater outside on the sidewalk where the picture of the person playing Juliet is displayed. She is African American, and above her picture are the words "Stunning new Juliet." Nana explains that she knows Rosalie Wilkins (the new Juliet) from Trinidad. She tells Grace that they are going to the ballet to see Rosalie Wilkins dance.

Seeing a black dancer play Juliet is liberating for Grace. She realizes she doesn't have to feel sad or defeated because of Natalie's remark. She could rise above it, and she does. When Grace returns to school and tries out for the part she is inspired by the new Juliet. More important, she responds to the rejection of her classmates with patience and kindness. They, including Raj and Natalie, vote her to be Peter Pan. "You were fantastic," whispers her friend, Natalie.

We do not know if the author is aware of the original biblical grace dynamic in this story. We do know that not all wretchedness is due to sin. In Grace's case, the unconditional love embedded in her name came through just the same. The Amazing Grace of this illustrated children's book and the Amazing Grace of the hymn do connect after all, and with a degree of irony.

The hymn has a reputation for being a "Negro spiritual," but its origin is anything but. For years the writer of the hymn, John Newman, was the captain of a slave ship. He was a party to the inhumane treatment of African men, women, and children. Then he heard a preacher in England tell about the grace of God and that changed him. He gave up his trade and was inspired to write the hymn. He had made the slaves feel wretched, but in the hymn *he* was the wretch. And since then, that word has a wide audience.

There is one other aspect to this story that should be examined. It may be misleading or disillusioning to think that anyone can be anything he or she wants to be. Real life is not always that accommodating. Grace could only pretend to be Joan of Arc or

Hiawatha or Peter Pan. When Charles Barkley of the National Basketball Association talks to African American children, he flat out tells them they have practically no chance of making it in professional basketball. High school, yes. College, maybe. The pros, no. He is right. Still, he urges them to stay in school, graduate, and go to college, and then become what they can. "Be all that you can be" is a phrase on which the U.S. Army does not have a franchise.

And along the way, there may be times when grace lifts us to an entirely new level of excellence just as it did for Grace and her classmates in the story. The grace of God inspires hope and greater effort. That grace is truly amazing because even when we fail God, God does not fail us.

Conversation Starters

1. What did you first think of when you saw the title of this book?

2. Is it fair to say there was something of biblical grace at work in the main character of this book, Grace?

3. Can anyone be anything they want to be in America or anywhere else?

Beatrice's Goat

by Page McBrier

illustrated by Lori Lohstoeter

40 pages

(New York: Atheneum, 2001)

This is a story of how a little in America goes a long way in Africa. When a family there receives the gift of a goat from friends they have never met, it sets up a chain reaction that includes nourishment, money for school, and a new house.

Our introduction to this true story is a picture that shows a young girl named Beatrice standing on the edge of a clearing. A few yards away is a group of children sitting on benches underneath a tree in Uganda deep in the hills of East Africa. They have carried the benches from their school that can be seen behind them. Beatrice would love to be a part of that group but has to content herself with pretending because she lacks both a uniform and book money necessary to go to school in her small village.

Then one day her mother tells her they are going to have a new member in the family—a goat. Beatrice wonders what a goat is. She has never seen one and isn't exactly enthused, unless it could hoe the field, start the charcoal fire each morning for cooking, or wash clothes in a nearby stream, all of which she has to do every day.

Of course the goat does not do the things Beatrice has in mind, but it does things she never dreamed of, such as providing milk, and two weeks after it arrives, giving birth to twins.

The goat is a gift from people who donate money to the Heifer Project International, an organization devoted to donating animals to poor families throughout the world. One of the stipulations is that the first offspring has to be given to another poor family. However, in Beatrice's case, since their goat had twins, the second kid was sold and the money was used to buy a steel roof for their house. Up until then their roof had been made of straw and when it rained it leaked.

Another by-product of the goat is milk. After the kids have been fed, and Beatrice adds some milk to her breakfast porridge, she sells a pail of milk to her friend Bunanc. He gives her a coin for each pail. Beatrice's first thought is to use the money to buy shirts and warm blankets for her brother and sister, but her mother has another idea. The money is enough to pay for her uniform and book money so she can go to school.

When I read of all the good that comes from goats, I wondered why Jesus placed them in a bad light. In his parable of the sheep and goats, the sheep are people who unselfishly help others, while the goats are concerned only for themselves. It was perhaps a cultural thing, but the labels have stuck. In Uganda, however, the parable of Jesus has to be told differently if the point is to be made.

In the story Beatrice's mother surrounds their little house with elephant plants that have tough leaves, providing the goat with a kind of pen in which to be kept. In reality, goats eat all kind of things, including cardboard boxes and bark from trees, so it would seem that the elephant leaves might also serve as a source of food. Goats are also fun pets, and it is hilarious to see them jump sideways, and rear up on their back legs ready to move forward and engage another goat with their horns.

The author notes that part of the money spent on purchasing the book will be given to Heifer Project International. The book is a good introduction to the Project, one that is well deserved considering all the good it does with what in America might be considered a rather small gift.

Hillary Rodham Clinton has written an afterword to the book in which she states that the Heifer Project International sent the author and illustrator to East Africa to research the story of the nine-year-old Ugandan girl. In Ms. Clinton's words, "It is a heartwarming reminder that families, wherever they live, can change their lives for the better. The story of Beatrice is an invitation to all of us to support those efforts that provide resources, educate families, and lift community spirit." The address for the Heifer Project International is 1015 Louisiana Street, Little Rock, AK 72202, or www.heifer.org.

Conversation Starters

1. Why is it that poor people in other countries can be so grateful with small gifts or can make them go so far in their lives?

2. Is it possible to have so many things that we lose the gift of gratitude or being thankful? If so why?

World Religions

Seven Blind Mice

by Ed Young

40 pages

(New York: Philomel Books, 1992)

Take an old folktale from India. Add echoes of the tale about three blind mice. Stir in a week of colors and you get a nicely illustrated story that suggests the whole is dependent upon all of its parts. It may even transcend them.

The word *blind* usually conjures up a person tapping a white cane on a curb, but it can also relate to all of us staring at something and not seeing it. Our minds are preoccupied. In this story it is clear that inner blindness is playing a part.

Seven blind mice find a strange Something out by their pond, and finding it there "they all ran home." Like the six men from Industan (India) in the original poem that inspired this story, they don't know it's an elephant. Indeed, what better animal to use as a metaphor of the Big Picture?

What is noteworthy about both the mice and the men is their curiosity. The mice are at first afraid and run home, but their curiosity gets the better of them, and one by one they return to identify the strange Something that so fascinates them. The only flaw in their curiosity is that they have to rely on interpretation, and as is true of interpretation, each has to rely on prior knowledge in order to render one.

The mice approach the Something in sequence. In other words, one of them goes first, and having blazed the trail the others follow. Fear of the unknown seems to motivate the initial reaction of the mice, but fortunately, in any field of endeavor, there is a pioneer who dares to explore the darkness.

For some reason the author of *Seven Blind Mice* includes all seven days of the week, and makes each mouse a different color. Both the days and the colors are missing from the original tale. A further departure from the original occurs when two of the mice touch the elephant. One touches the leg and concludes that it is a pillar, whereas in the original tale told by John Saxe, an Englishman who had spent time in India, the one who touches the leg perceives it to be a tree trunk. Similarly, Thursday's mouse is shown on the forehead of the elephant. He decides he is on a cliff, whereas in the original there is no forehead contact, but instead the Hindu touches the side of the animal, which suggests he is feeling a wall.

Four of the parts of the elephant, however, are the same in both stories. The trunk is regarded as a snake, the tusk a spear, the ear a fan, and the tail a rope. Each one draws upon prior understandings of and names for snakes, spears, fans, and ropes. In a sense they could hardly do otherwise, and while we are thoroughly accustomed to calling a thing that crawls on its belly a snake, we call it that only because someone at some point in time so named it, and we got used to that name. It is true with everything that has a name.

Both tales reach a point where the participants discuss what they find, and they do so animatedly—they argue. The Hindu poem is fetching because of its rhyme. It is as follows:

And so these men of Industan disputed long and
    loud,
Each in his own opinion exceeding stiff and strong;

Though each was partly in the right, all were in the
wrong.

What is going on in this argumentative phase of the story-
poem is partly ignorance and partly arrogance. The men do not
listen to each other long enough to ask questions. They each
assume that their "bit" is the whole of it, and similar assump-
tions have served to plague the human race to this day. Perhaps
it is our human need for certainty. Entertaining uncertainty is
not something we can do, unless we are scientists who by train-
ing are able to live with it.

The Hindu tale does not resolve this dispute, and even
takes it one step further than Ed Young does. At the same time
Young adds a resolution to the story in the form of the Seventh
Mouse who, having listened to the other six, presumably concludes that they may all be wrong, but that there is no reason to
settle for that ending to the situation. Why Number Seven ven-
tures forth on Sunday may be symbolic or it may not. Young does
not help us at this point. What he does do is have Number
Seven run up and down and all around the strange Something
and putting the pieces of the puzzle together he "sees" that,
indeed, they each described a part of what is an elephant.

Mouse Number Seven might have been stimulated by the
differences his mousy friends exhibited in their argument, or
was one of those rare creatures who, unable to live with uncertainty, takes all the information available and tries to make sense
of the situation. The vital ingredient to the mind of the Seventh
Mouse is that he was not afraid to think. Thought enters the
arena where the whole is equal only to the sum of its parts, or
transcends it. It deciphers the Big Picture.

We conclude this description of the tale by sharing the last
verse in the original poem. We do so in part because it is cus-
tomary even by those who refer to the original or quote from it,
to leave the last verse out. There is a bias against religion in

many quarters, but in this case it is that very bias that gives the poem meaning. The final verse reads as follows:

> So often in theological wars, the disputants, it does
> seem,
> Rail on in utter ignorance of what each other means
> And prate about an Elephant not one of them has
> seen!

In the original poem the elephant is a metaphor for God, a God that silently sustains the universe. The closest Young gets to God is that he capitalizes the Something that is out by the pond, but whether he has the Creator in mind by doing that we do not know.

Blindness becomes particularly poignant in the area of religion. Yet, no religious person of whatever stripe or day of the week has seen God. All have to take someone's words for what they believe, and that holds true for those whose claim is that this Unseen God has gotten in touch with them—not our touching God—like a voice from another planet.

The assumption that our religion or religious insight is the whole of it has killed a lot of people, and is still doing so. Were we to do what Mouse Number Seven did and listen to the others and allow what we hear to motivate us to seek further, we would step into the quiet dimension of the Big Picture. The Hindu story does this with unsettling authority, but so does the tale of seven blind mice. The message is partly in the structure of the story, but the Big Picture is Something that beckons in many fields of human endeavor, not just in religion.

Conversation Starters

1. Why do you think the author/illustrator, Ed Young, included the days of the week and different colors for the mice?

2. Why is it hard to truly listen when we believe in something so strongly?

3. Do you hear any echoes from the elephant today?

Religions Explained

by Anita Ganeri

72 pages

(New York: Henry Holt, 1997)

> *The elephant from* Seven Blind Mice *puts in an appearance in this book, but as God, not as a metaphor. By raising questions and probing beneath surface explanations we get to the Big Picture, the heart of what God is like.*

Anita Ganeri provides pictures and verbal descriptions of nearly twenty-five world religions, with enough information to cause us to seek further explanations. For example, because there are many gods and goddesses referred to, it is natural to wonder how they came about, for mathematically there can be only one of infinite capacity. Fortunately we do not have to read very far for some initial clues.

In what the author refers to as ancient religions, there are ample reasons in the natural world for believing that God can be harsh. Floods, storms, or drought all point to a deity angry about something who needs to be appeased or pleased. People of early religions were quite certain that such natural eruptions never just happened but were the result of an ancestor or god who was upset. Thus prayers and beautiful temples were responses to the threat of violent eruptions in the physical world. The author does not say this, but the responses are a kind of flattery even though they are motivated by fear. The Aztecs and Incas, for example, were convinced the gods could be influenced by offerings and sacrifices, and thus they would feed human hearts to them. The Greeks held festivals in honor of their gods to gain their favor. At the root of these motivations was fear of consequences of disobedience.

The book explains that belief in one God is important to some religions. However, this deity also gets angry when his laws have been broken. Disruptions in the natural world are often seen as a form of punishment here too. Still, the prayer and worship response is similar. Indeed, both the response of God and our responses to God suggest that those of the ancient religions are still with us. Thus, teachers of world religions are more inclined to refer to fear as a *basic* response—not an ancient one.

Included among the diverse names for God in world religions is a word that is strictly impersonal. It is called the Tao, a force that is active in the world, bringing autocratic monarchs and others to their knees. In Taoism, the sanest response is to live in harmony with the Tao, meaning a life devoid of riches and self-glorification. However, again we bump into a temperamental side to this force that needs to be taken seriously, so in Taoism, temples and rituals are important. Nonetheless, what surfaces here is that when the priorities and power are present, the Creator apparently does not mind who gets the credit.

Religion has a long-standing reputation for demanding obedience from its followers, and in this book that emphasis is repeated over and over again. The book does a fine job of describing the origins, beliefs, and festivals of religion, but when it comes to why this focus is on obedience it draws a blank. Instead, we find lists of rules to be obeyed. Even in "ancient religions" such as those of Egypt and Mesopotamia the author notes that "it was important to obey the gods and not to make them angry," though we do not know what the rules were.

In Hinduism, one of the oldest religions, the laws known as Dharma are related to the four castes. In Buddhism there is the Eightfold Path, and in Islam there are Five Pillars. In Judaism there are the Ten Commandments, and a host of lesser rules regarding food preparation and consumption, ceremonies, and personal relationships found in Leviticus, the Book of the Law. In response to this, Judaism split into three basic groups—Orthodox, Conservative, and Reform—with the latter advocating the tailoring of religion to the needs of contemporary life and times.

In Christianity, the Ten Commandments are also honored, but they are summed up in loving God and one's neighbor as one's self. The Golden Rule is found in the Gospels of Jesus, but it is a "rule" found in most major religions, suggesting a common origin that transcends humanity and regions. Christianity also presents itself as the most difficult religion because in the Gospels Jesus insists that we are to be perfect, as "your heavenly Father is perfect."

His admonition may have been shared in order to puncture the pride of the Pharisees and other religious leaders, but it confronts anyone who reads the Sermon on the Mount in Matthew's Gospel. The need to win God's approval by way of obedience remains. Fortunately, Christianity includes a way of forgiveness and an accent on grace, though this often is lost sight of as people try to live up to the law's demands.

The reason for laws, rules, statutes, regulations, or whatever they are called is not noted in this book, but it is an obvious question, since it is a theme religions have in common. Theologians suggest that there is an "oughtness" in humanity because the Creator is holy and, as Jesus suggested, God is perfect. God cannot help but be this way, and it is reasonable to assume that the many efforts to please God spring from the belief that God not only demands obedience but will also punish any lack of it.

This punishment reaches its ultimate in the threat of hell. In Islam the Day of Judgment is strongly emphasized. It is also highlighted in Zoroastrianism as noted in this book. However, omitted in this book is the fascinating manner in which Zoroastrianism also has a resurrection from the dead for all people, including those in hell. It is a meaningful prelude to the concept of resurrection in Christianity.

A theme that is integral to various religions, but conspicuous by its absence in this book, is social justice. The language on Planet Earth that brings attention to bear upon the poor was first introduced through the Hebrew prophets, Isaiah and Amos. It was then picked up by Islam and is embedded in two of its Five Pillars (giving alms and fasting in the month of Ramadan to show solidarity with the poor). This has been carried forward by a spinoff from Islam known as Baha'i, in which the elimination of both poverty and wealth is advocated. It is also an important ingredient in Taoism's aversion to material riches and self-glory.

Islam's focus on social justice for the poor is omitted in much of the news during coverage of the war on terrorism. The news media carries much detail about smart bombs, our effectiveness in this war, and lifting up the *evil* of those responsible for the collapse of the World Trade Towers. Often missing is the reason why anyone would sacrifice himself or herself in this attack. To bring out the role of social justice would have set the United States up for criticism.

The book notes how there are opportunities for seeking and receiving forgiveness for disobedience in some religions. In Hinduism it is bathing in the river Ganges, thereby washing away one's sins. There is also the nature of one of Hinduism's major deities, Vishnu, and his incarnation, Krishna. That *nature* is forgiving, and in the story of Krishna in the Bhagavad Gita, the word *grace* appears several times.

In biblical Judaism there is a sacrificial system, along with a Day of Atonement, which is observed to this day. Islam declares that Allah is all forgiving, but while it is so stated, it does not emerge as a practice in that religion. When we come to Christianity, the death of Jesus for the sins of the world rises up to greet us, along with the focus on grace in the writings of Paul. In this book forgiveness is lifted up as the purpose for the Eucharist, or Lord's Supper, but grace (forgiveness) and its unconditionality in the writings of Paul does not receive the attention he gives to it. It is interesting to note that the unconditionality of mercy shows up in a religion such as Christianity wherein the demand for perfection is articulated. Worship is an appropriate response to this grace, but the motivation is praise and gratitude, not fear.

Conversation Starters

1. How do you feel about the idea that mathematically there can only be one God?

2. How do you account for the presence of laws in all religions?

3. What does this do to religion's reputation?

4. Why is unconditional mercy (grace) necessary in relation to religious laws?

And Still the Turtle Watched

by Sheila MacGill-Callahan

illustrated by Barry Moser

32 pages

(New York: Dial Books, 1991)

> *In keeping with the religious beliefs of the First Delaware Nation, a turtle is carved out of rock. He watches the people. He serves as the eyes and ears of the Unseen Spirit— Manitou. Time and people hurt the turtle until a stranger comes to the rescue.*

Among the many religious beliefs of the American Indian nations, there is one they have in common. It is the idea of a Great Spirit. Its name might vary, but people do not pray to it or speak to it, and for such reasons it also came to be known as the Great Silence. The Delaware Nation called it Manitou, which means the Father of All.

One other religious belief the first Americans share is animism, the belief that spirits animate all of nature—sun, earth, animals, trees, and even stones. Since no one ever spoke to the Great Spirit, or heard from the Great Silence, animism brings the Spirit closer to home. It is all around, embodied in nature.

Thus, it is not unnatural that a member of the Delaware Nation decided to carve a turtle on the top of a large rock. Whether turtles make any noise at all I do not know. The turtle seems to specialize in silence, in just looking, a perfect symbol of the Great Spirit of Silence. The turtle's task is to watch. He is the eyes and ears of Manitou.

One can say that animism is a form of incarnation, a form in which various facets of nature take on life. In the case of the turtle, each summer children were brought to his site to greet him and pay him homage.

This went on for years while the rain, wind, snow, and dust slowly but surely wore the turtle down. Perhaps he was carved out of sandstone that is softer than granite. As time wore him away, fewer children came to greet him until finally they no longer came at all, and the turtle thought, "Have I watched badly?" This development made him sad.

However, there was more sadness to come, one being in the form of machines that "killed the forest" by chopping down the trees and putting cement over the ground with buildings on them—with lights that made it harder to see the stars of Manitou. The turtle did not understand what was going on.

It seemed to the turtle that Manitou no longer heard him. The notion of the turtle serving as an intercessor shows up here. He brings the concerns of the people to the Father of All. The turtle felt so bad that he wept. We are reminded of the shortest verse in the Bible, the one that simply notes, "Jesus wept." The incarnational nature of the turtle in relation to the Spirit of Silence is also not lost in this story.

Then to add woe to misery, one day some older children discovered the rock upon which the turtle was carved. At first the turtle was happy to see them. But then they did a strange thing. They pointed something round at him and he felt a cool wetness cover his face. Soon he could no longer see. It was graffiti, something some teenagers spray on lots of things. We call such an act vandalism.

More time turns into history until one day another stranger comes trekking through the hills looking for a sign that the Delaware Nation had been there. Eventually he comes upon the turtle and he knows instantly what he is. He has heard the story. He knows about Manitou. The turtle, of course, cannot see him, but he knows something is happening. The man arranges to move the large rock and the turtle and at first this frightens the turtle. He has never moved in all his years on the top of the rock. Then he is jostled and bounced, which happens to most of us when we ride in a truck.

The turtle's final destiny, however, is a fitting conclusion to this story. It was a museum, where one of the first things done was to remove the graffiti. The turtle could see again, and both children and adults could come and see him and read about him The history of the turtle had not been lost, and now people could see how the turtle watches them with great care.

If you happen to visit New York City or live there you can see the turtle at the Watson Building in the New York Botanical Garden. "Weathered and worn, its features are no longer distinct, although its basic shape and nature can still be seen by those who know and believe."

Conversation Starters

1. Why were the first Americans so sensitive to nature and the physical world?

2. Would this sensitivity have taken place had it not been for their having a strong spiritual perception or belief?

3. What things can you do to carry on the first Americans' concern that nature be enjoyed and not ruined?

Mother Teresa: Sister to the Poor

by Patricia Reilly Giff

64 pages

(New York: Puffin Books, 1987)

> *Mother Teresa's name is well known throughout the world, but India knows it best because in at least one way she changed that country. It all happened because of what she endured and why. It is the story behind her story, one we should all know.*

What I first remember reading about India was how members of the untouchable caste move throughout the city streets each morning to pick up the bodies. The dead are from their caste. It is basic to the Hindu belief that their condition is a punishment for something they did in their previous life. It is a belief known as *karma*, which means the law of deeds. If someone lives in a nice house and has a good life, it is because that person is being rewarded for a previous life. But the poor, and especially the poorest of the poor, are paying for their previous lives by suffering.

Sister Teresa's first contact with the poor in India was a glimpse of their tin roofs from her bedroom window in St. Mary's Convent, a Roman Catholic school set in the midst of the Moti

Jheel slum on the fringe of Calcutta. The convent, surrounded by high walls for protection, was like an oasis. She lived there and taught geography and history to rich Bengali girls. She was an excellent teacher and became principal of the school, but something was wrong. She had come to India to work among the poor, and instead she lived in a beautiful stone building with a lovely, peaceful lake in front of it. The high walls hid most of the horror outside.

Sister Teresa had first heard of the poor of India as a fifteen-year-old girl in Skopje, Macedonia. She began thinking about them. Becoming a nun was a way to respond to poverty. At first she tried putting the idea out of her mind but it would not go away. She began to believe that God was calling her to go to India.

In the fall of 1928 she boarded a ship for Darjeeling, a warm resort city nestled at the foot of the snowy Himalaya Mountains. There she learned Hindi and Bengali and taught children in a little one-room school on the convent grounds. She made her vows and became a bride of Christ, symbolized by wearing a thin gold circle on the third finger of her right hand. She also chose two new names. The first was Mary. All sisters choose this name to honor the Mother of Christ. The second was Teresa, the name of a Carmelite nun who believed in doing the smallest, humble tasks for the love of God.

From the vantage point of the convent on the edge of Calcutta, the poor in the Moti Jheel slum were right outside her window, but they "seemed like a million miles away." Sister Teresa felt she had to go to them, that God was giving her a "call within a call" to live and work among the poor. On August 16, 1948, she took off the black habit of the Loreto Order, donned a simple white cotton sari (the dress of Indian women), pinned a small crucifix on her left shoulder, and left the convent.

When she entered the slum, she saw people living in drain pipes, in gutters, in broken-down cars, and on the streets in the midst of sacred cows and other animals, with human waste piled high on the roads for lack of drainage. And with those kinds of living conditions came rats, sickness, and premature death, all sanctioned by the belief in karma. It was this belief that Mother Teresa helped to change, and she did it by living among the poor, living like them, and ministering to them. Because to her, this place was also like the place where a baby had been born in Bethlehem many centuries before, a place some call a cave, others a stable, though most commonly referred to as a manger, a feeding trough for beasts of burden.

She began by doing what she had done inside the convent—teaching. However, she had no schoolroom, no books, no paper, and no pencils. Finding an open spot between some huts, she began tracing Bengali letters in the ground with a small stick. One by one out of curiosity nearby slum children walked over to see what she was doing. They crouched on the ground beside her, and that was her first class. The subject was cleanliness and it included her washing them with soap and water. Most of them had never seen a piece of soap, and water, being scarce, was not used for bathing.

Word of what she was doing began to spread. Friends of St. Mary's brought her things for a school and a priest friend helped her find a place to stay. It was owned by a Roman Catholic teacher who gave her a room without rent and some food. She added a small chair and a box for a desk, and hung a picture of the Blessed Mother on the wall.

Word also spread in the slums, and after teaching children during the day, she began helping the adult sick. She would rise at 4:30 A.M., attend Mass, and then begin her work. Someone provided a place where she could set up a dispensary. More sick people began coming to her and so did the hungry. Soon the numbers were overwhelming. When asked how she was able to do it, she said she did not think of the crowds, but only of the one in front of her she was helping. When asked how she could stand the stench of human waste, she answered that when she worked with someone ill, she believed she was meeting God. Every cup of water, every scrap of food was being given to the Lord. Their misery was his and his was hers. This was the faith that kept her going.

Soon one of her pupils at St. Mary's came to join her, then another, and it was the beginning of the Missionaries of Charity. From then on she was called Mother.

More students arrived. The number of students grew to ten and there was no room for them. Another place had to be found, and from another priest it was learned that a man who owned a house was leaving Calcutta. He was a Muslim but he ended up giving his home to her. He said, "I got this house from God and I give it back to him." In February 1953 she moved the sisters into their new home. Its address, 54A Lower Circular Road, was to become famous all over the world.

She proceeded to take in the dying, giving them a place where they could be made as comfortable as possible and where they could see that they were not alone. Mother Teresa went to the City Hall and town officials agreed to let her use the room in the back of a Hindu temple dedicated to Kali, the Hindu goddess of death. After the sisters cleaned the place, the dying were brought there, some literally dragged inside where they could be helped. The sisters washed them, removed maggots from their wounds, and gave them water and soup. "They are Jesus," Mother Teresa said of the dying.

The complaints began. This was not the way to treat those who were being punished for their previous life. Some accused her of wanting to convert them to Catholicism. Others threw sticks at the sisters. The neighbors sent a policeman to the temple to remove her, but when he saw what she was doing he just shook his head and left. When a man dying of cholera was brought in and it was learned that he was a Hindu priest, an upper caste person, people's views began to change. Neighborhood women came to the temple to help. Doctors came too, when they could, helping diagnose illnesses and suggesting treatments. Supplies also showed up, given by people who heard what was happening. When some of the dying got well, it was viewed as miraculous.

Skeptics of her work said that it touched so few. What needed to be done, they said, was to change society's views toward those who suffer, to change Hindu beliefs themselves. Although Mother Teresa always saw this as belonging to the political realm—one she shied away from—in a way she did change societal views, even Hindu beliefs, by working with individuals. She demonstrated that karma was not an irreversible fate. It was as if Christ entered into the lives of the people of Calcutta with a different response, one of love and care for the poor and suffering, and this she did without trying to convert them to Christianity or Catholicism.

Sister Teresa not only became the mother of Calcutta, but also the mother of India. After she received the Nobel prize for peace in 1979, some newspapers in India reported, "The Mother of Bengal has become the Mother of the World."

Conversation Starters

1. What indications were there in Mother Teresa's life that God was guiding her?

2. What motivations for her work do you regard as the most important?

3. In what ways did she have an impact on India—and on the whole world?

Music

Handel, Who Knew What He Liked

by M. T. Anderson

illustrated by Kevin Hawkes

48 pages

(Cambridge, MA: Candlewick Press, 2001)

> *Handel was a man who knew what he liked and did just that. This often meant persuading others to do something they themselves may not have wanted to do, but eventually they came around to his point of view.*

Handel's father was a doctor, and what he wanted his son to do was to make money. The son, on the other hand, liked music, so much so that one night he smuggled a clavichord upstairs to the attic without his parents knowing it. There he taught himself how to play. It's an instrument much like a piano, except that the strings have to be struck by hammers held in one's hands.

On another occasion his father told him he could not accompany him in his carriage to see his brother, who was working in a distant castle. Handel ran for miles behind the coach until his father looked out, saw him, stopped, and let him ride the rest of the way. The illustrations in this book are wonderful and the one showing him keeping up with the coach is really quite funny.

At the castle the duke heard the organ playing, but could not see anyone on the bench. When he was told it was Handel, he recognized the boy's ability and supported him along with having to convince Handel's father that it was the right thing to do.

In Hamburg, Germany, Handel and another musician—Mattheson—became good friends. Mattheson wrote his own operas and invited himself to be the star. He would die on stage halfway into the opera, then run down to conduct the second half, usually having to elbow Handel out of the conductor's place. One night Handel refused to budge and Mattheson challenged him to a duel. Fortunately for the world, one of Handel's buttons prevented a sword's thrust from reaching his heart, and later that evening the two went out to dinner.

Handel wrote Italian opera and got around the religious authorities in Rome by setting religious texts to music. Indeed, he knew what he liked and went after it.

In 1710 Handel journeyed to England, where he was encouraged by the queen to write opera, which he did often using special effects, such as releasing live birds to fly around the theater. English people did not like opera, thinking, Why sing it if you can say it? Handel decided to persuade them by having the singers stab each other. It worked. English people started to enjoy opera.

He composed his famous *Water Music* for King George I and played it from a boat carrying an orchestra while the king sailed nearby on his own boat. The king loved it so much he asked to hear it three times.

One performance was a disaster. Designed to bring together the kings of England and Germany, who had been at war, it featured fireworks and music written by Handel, but the palace caught fire as rockets and pinwheels exploded inside the building.

To silence critics of opera, Handel hired famous singers, but they became jealous if one got more arias to sing than another. One time two singers got into a fistfight on stage, but the people loved it.

At one point Handel was challenged by another composer, John Gay, whose operas were set in London, sung in English, and woven around merchants and thieves, instead of Handel's kings and queens from exotic places. Rather than arias, Gay used popular songs. People began to laugh at Handel's efforts at serious music.

When he was unable to win over the English people to Italian opera, it was a blow to him. He was about to give up when he was asked to do a benefit concert for some Irish orphanages. The music he wrote for it was called *Messiah*. The words were taken from the Bible, and words and notes came to him so rapidly he often left his lunch uneaten. It was as if he were possessed or inspired. He finished it in twenty-one days. This was in 1741.

The *Messiah* inspired the wealthy to give much money to the orphanages. Both singers and hearers alike were captured by its melodiousness and it was a huge success. It is still popular even today at Christmas and Easter. The most exciting part is the "Hallelujah Chorus." A tradition began during Handel's time that the audience would stand while it was sung; this continues in many performances to this day.

Handel stopped writing Italian operas to write oratorios in English in which he made the words and music give life to each other. The *Messiah* is the most famous of his oratorios. Once an orchestra of 500 and a chorus of 4,000 performed it.

In 1757 Handel started to lose his sight and soon had to excuse himself from performing. Two years later he died and was buried in Westminster Abbey in London.

Some special features of this picture-book biography appear at the end. One is a chronology of Handel's life. Another is a discography, a list of compact discs, and a third is suggestions for further reading. Throughout the book the illustrations and the "sidebars" of information join in the humorous approach that makes this book well liked by both young and older readers.

Conversation Starters

1. How do we understand the inspiration that came to Handel in the *Messiah*?

2. How do we explain the emergence of talent like Handel's? Where does it come from?

3. How do you feel about the observation directed at opera, that is, why sing it if you can say it?

Mole Music

by David McPhail

32 pages

(New York: Henry Holt, 1999)

> *Underground usually means something sinister or secretive, but in this story what originates under the ground has a beneficial influence on the world above it, thanks to Mole.*

Although it is long, I am using the word *anthropomorphism* to introduce this story. It means the attaching of human qualities to nonhuman characters or creatures, in this case, a mole. He lives and works in a tunnel beneath a tree. The first illustration shows him expanding his home. He wears a headlamp to see what he is doing, and he is about to bring a pickaxe down on the earth to loosen it. A shovel and a wheelbarrow are also in the picture, to be used as he digs. In the second picture he is sitting in an easy chair watching TV in what might be called his living room—all this in a little tunnel under the ground.

Mole gets the feeling that something is missing in his life until he hears a violinist play beautiful music at a concert on his television set. He decides he wants to play like that and so he sends away for a violin. Three weeks later it arrives by mail.

At this point the reader is introduced to a small tree just above his tunnel. Its roots have pierced the ground and are dangling in the space that is Mole's living room and practice area.

The first draw of the bow across the strings of his new violin produces a screech that travels up the root system through the thin trunk and frightens two birds that are sitting in the branches. It is not easy to learn how to play a violin, as some readers or their parents may know, and a screech may very well be the first sound the would-be violinist produces. Not only do the birds fly away, but the tree's branches also droop as if Mole's noise drains the life out of them.

The reader turns the page only to find out that years have gone by—a little literary license here. Mole is still practicing and his noise has become music. He has greatly improved, and at this point we need to acknowledge that practice may not make one perfect, but it truly pays off. Persistence spells s-u-c-c-e-s-s. Mole is much happier now that he is able to make music with his violin.

The tree has come back to life and the birds have come back to the tree. The author/artist shows musical notes traveling up the roots through the trunk that is much wider now and out through the branches covered with leaves.

On several pages the pictures are split-level. Each shows the tree above ground and Mole's tunnel/home below it. At this point the split-level picture shows a small group of peasants cutting the grain that has grown in the field surrounding the tree. One person is holding a scythe, another a rake, and still others are bundling the grain to carry it away. Before they leave for the day they hear music. It seems to be coming from the tree. They sit down to enjoy it. Mole is playing in his tunnel, all the time not realizing his music is traveling to the surface and is heard by some people.

On the very next page the author introduces a key word in his story, the word *imagine*. It enters Mole's mind. He imagines himself playing before a large audience, including presidents and queens, and sure enough, around the tree above him there is a man who looks like George Washington sitting on a horse, and on the other side of the tree is a king sitting on a throne.

The reader may also start wondering at this point whether the people gathered at the tree are real or if they are all in Mole's head. On the front flyleaf of the book the publisher has written that "even though he [Mole] plays alone, in the privacy of his underground home, his music has an effect on others that is more magical than Mole will ever know." That suggests that at least some of the people who hear the music coming from the tree are real people. Whether that pertains to the people in all the pictures the reader might want to discuss with someone, for the word *imagine* is still in Mole's head.

Mole imagines his music taking away anger and sadness. He pictures his music changing the world, and here above his home two armies are poised, each on opposite sides of the tree on two hills, ready to do battle. Lances are held by soldiers on horseback on one side and swords are in the hands of riders on the other side.

The armies charge down their hills toward each other as Mole laughs at his thought that his music might change the world, removing anger and sadness. However, when the two armies reach the vicinity of the tree they stop. One army throws away its lances and the other its swords. The tree has acted like an antenna, broadcasting Mole's music to the world around it. It alters the mood of the soldiers so they climb down from their horses and embrace each other, shake hands, and smiles appear on their faces where just before grim features revealed how they felt.

The words that leap out at the reader at this point are from Mole. He reflects again how silly it is that he thinks his music could change the world "when no one has even heard it." These words imply that all the time Mole's imagination has been working overtime, real people have assembled by the tree above him and are being moved by Mole's music, without his realizing it is happening.

He is not on TV but he does have an audience, and perhaps there is a word of encouragement in this story for all who don't see the fruit of their efforts. It is that, should they continue, they, too, may influence other people and change the way others look at life, even the world in which they live, though they may never know it.

Conversation Starters

1. Were the people by the tree real or a product of Mole's imagination?

2. What motivated Mole to learn to play the violin?

3. What incentives are there to practice?

Beethoven Lives Upstairs

by Barbara Nichol

illustrated by Scott Cameron

48 pages

(New York: Orchard Books, 1993)

> *At first young Christoph is put off by the old man's eccentricity. Gradually, through letters from his uncle, he gains compassion for him, and a relationship with Ludwig von Beethoven develops.*

What would you think if an old man rented a room at your house, and he howled and made other loud noises? Ten-year-old Christoph thought a mad man had moved in. The man even had four pianos; he had sawed the legs off of one of them, so it sat on the floor. Then, there was the drip. It came from the ceiling, and when Christoph crept upstairs to peer in the door, he saw why. The old man Ludwig was pouring water over his head in the living room and it pooled beneath his feet on the floor. (The author notes how the composer had headaches and leaves the reader to conclude the water is the treatment.)

Then there was the messenger who delivered a note from the prince. It said that if Beethoven was working he was not to be disturbed. The old man must be terrible to frighten a prince, thought the young lad.

Fortunately, Christoph had an uncle who provided some understanding. To Christoph's first letter about the mad man upstairs, his Uncle Karl replied that there must be reasons why Beethoven acted as he did. In another letter he informed his nephew that Beethoven had an unhappy childhood. His father was also a musician, but one who liked to drink. He would come home in the middle of the night, get Ludwig out of bed, and make him practice until dawn (or so he said).

Uncle Karl connected Beethoven's temper with the frustration he felt over being deaf. It began when the composer was eight years old and was unable to hear high notes. Uncle Karl planted another seed of understanding when he told Christoph that Beethoven "hears no music, not even his own."

Deafness might also explain his sawing off the legs of one piano. When Beethoven sat on the floor and played, he could feel the vibration of the notes through the floorboards. As the correspondence between Christoph and Karl proceeds, things began to fall into place for the boy.

Although the author writes that Beethoven "hears no music, not even his own," that is not quite accurate. Beethoven heard the tunes in his head, and perhaps this is true for all gifted composers. So it would be more accurate to say he never heard anyone play his music. He could not go to the piano and hear it, or play it over and over to get the notes and chords just right. This had to be done inside his mind. That was the unique thing about Beethoven. When Mozart wanted to hear what his music sounded like on the piano, all he had to do was sit down and play it. Not so Beethoven.

He presents a magnificent example of inspiration. He would go to a party and play a new piece of music without one note to guide him. It was spontaneous, impromptu. The tune was hiding in his head, waiting to emerge. There were no electrodes fastened to his head piping these tunes into his brain so he could transmit them onto paper for posterity.

For a curious mind the origin of spontaneous, beautiful music generates the possibility of God being involved. In this book there is no indication or hint that Beethoven credits a Source, but that doesn't rule it out. If there is such a thing as inspiration, it begs a source.

There is a moment in the story that stretches one's belief capacity. It is when two conductors direct an orchestra that is playing one of Beethoven's pieces. (This is shown in a companion video of the book.) When the musical score ends, the orchestra stops playing, and one of the conductors stops directing, but Beethoven keeps on waving his arms. Actually, if we stop to think about it, the two conductors would have to be in perfect sync. Otherwise the orchestra members would not know whom to follow. But if they were in such perfect synchronization, why have *two* conductors? Perhaps they did it once, at Beethoven's insistence, and given that seed of truth, a myth grew up around it.

I would like to underscore the value of the two companion pieces to this book, a videotape and a cassette tape. It was sheer delight to hear them after reading the book. (They can probably be taken out at a public library.) Music has to be heard to be appreciated. Describing music cannot do it justice. This is especially true with regard to the hauntingly beautiful melodies of Beethoven. And hearing the music on either tape would be a great way to inspire a youngster to listen to more of it, perhaps even to take piano lessons and practice. And if a parent wishes to quietly create some distance from rock music these selected pieces of Beethoven might help. Hearing these tunes is an essential element in learning about Ludwig von Beethoven. It injects the three-letter word *a-w-e* into the picture.

Our grandson was five years old when we gave him a tape entitled "Classical Child." He used to play it in a little tape recorder. One day we went for a picnic in Boston Common, and he carried it around playing the classical pieces of Mozart and Beethoven. People would stop and stare at this little boy enjoying classical music. They were used to loud rock or jazz. To this day classical pieces are his favorites.

In the book, when Christoph heard Beethoven pounding away on the pianos upstairs, he did not get the melodies, but when he went to the performance of Beethoven's *Ninth Symphony* he at last heard the beauty of the man's music and his appreciation for the older man soared. Christoph felt such joy coming from the music that he concluded it must have been dammed up inside of Beethoven's head and perhaps that was one of the reasons for his temper and frustration. The composer wanted to get it all down on paper so that others could enjoy what he was hearing in his mind.

Conversation Starters

1. Where do the beautiful, simple tunes that some composers share with the world come from?

2. Why is rock music so different from the simple melodious sounds that come from the classical composers?

3. Why in this case was understanding necessary in order to experience compassion?

Sing to the Stars

by Mary Brigid Barrett

illustrated by Sandra Speidel

32 pages

(Boston: Little, Brown, 1994)

> *A former classical pianist sits in front of his laundromat, no longer playing piano, until Ephram, a young boy, walks by carrying his violin case. Their friendship helps Mr. Washington come out of grief-induced retirement.*

We may all be aware of how people who are blind seem to be able to hear very well. Balthazar Washington is one of those who have 20/20 ears. (He was probably named after one of the Wise Men, and Mr. Washington is, indeed, a wise man.) He sits in his folding chair on the sidewalk in front of his laundromat.

Young Ephram approaches him. Mr. Washington, looking straight ahead behind his dark glasses, asks, "How are you today, Ephram?"

A perplexed Ephram asks how he knows that he's walking by, and from the response he learns that here is a blind man who can tell a person's steps by their rhythm. To the older man's ears, Ephram has the song of life in his steps. Mr. Washington can even tell whether Ephram is happy or sad by his walk. Most of the time when the boy comes from his violin lesson he is happy.

Ephram likes to play the violin, and he likes to practice on his roof after supper as darkness envelops the city. Mr. Washington, who opens his windows on hot summer evenings, hears him and wryly observes how he thinks it is Mr. Bach letting some beautiful notes slip out from his heavenly studio.

Mr. Washington tells Ephram about an open mike benefit concert at the park and urges the young protégé to play. He tells Ephram that "music speaks best when someone listens." It's a nice remark and he doesn't realize how it is going to come back to visit him.

Ephram learns from his grandma that Mr. Washington was a classical pianist who once was able to "flash" across the keys, earning him the nickname "Flash Fingers Washington." When he lost his sight in a car accident, along with his daughter, he never played the piano again.

It doesn't take Ephram long to get to Mr. Washington and make a deal with him: if he plays the piano at the concert, Ephram will play his violin. He doesn't know if Mr. Washington will do it but Ephram goes to the concert and sits with his grandma in the front row. They save a seat for the piano player, but as the concert starts to wind down there still is no Mr. Washington.

Suddenly there's a power shortage and the lights go out. Ephram decides that's his cue to play when he hears Mr. Washington say, "It's always dark up on the roof...isn't it Ephram?" Ephram heads for the stage to play some of his grandma's hymn tunes. He invites Mr. Washington to join him and says, "Music speaks best when someone listens." Mr. Washington can't argue with that since he had already said it to Ephram.

Ephram asks him if he knows "Amazing Grace," and Mr. Washington replies, "Ephram, I was playing 'Amazing Grace' when you were a thought in the good Lord's mind." Mr.

Washington places his hand on Ephram's shoulder and says, "Ready, son?"

Gramma warns them to be careful climbing onto the stage, but Ephram notes how Mr. Washington sees in the dark.

With that the story ends, leaving me with many thoughts, one of which is that both musicians are quite able, due to different circumstances, to play in the dark. They have that in common and the discovery comes to both of them at the concert setting in the park.

Another thought that formed in my mind was that it would have been appropriate to end the story with that line from the hymn, "Amazing Grace," "I was blind but now I see." It could be related to Mr. Washington's words of encouragement to Ephram, setting another stage. While he lost a daughter, he gained a son, and the relationship based on friendship gave Mr. Washington a new reason for living, one that brought his ability to play the piano out of mothballs.

Conversation Starters

1. Do you know anyone who is blind who has developed a keen sense of hearing, or have you ever heard of this happening?

2. In what sense might Mr. Washington and Ephram have had a bond of friendship before they even met?

3. Why has "Amazing Grace" become a kind of national hymn, played in many places outside of a church building?

4. Based on the way the story unfolds, do you think Mr. Washington sort of adopts Ephram or are his words "ready, son?" just a general type of reference?